MY LIFE AS A BIRDER

A Collection of Stories from Attu to Zambia

HARRIET DAVIDSON

Davidson Devendorf Publishing
Brooklyn, New York

Previously printed and distributed to friends and family
with the title *A Modern Viking in the World of Birds*.

Versions of the stories "In Search of the Ross's Gull,"
"Two for the Price of One," "How to Find a Great Gray Owl,"
"Sharp Eyes Keep Sharp Lookout for Sharp-Tail,"
"Arizona Heat Wave," "Baby Barn Owls," and "Tanzania"
were previously published in the Port Huron, Michigan, *Times Herald*.

Versions of the stories "The Key West Quail Dove Bird Chase,"
"Sharp Eyes Keep Sharp Lookout for Sharp-Tail," and
"The Dry Tortugas: A Tropical Paradise" were previously
published in *Bird Watcher's Digest*.

The text of this book was set in Cochin.
Manufactured in the United States of America

CONTENTS

Part III: Alaska

Part IV: Narrow Escapes

Part V: The Amazon

Part VI: Around the World

Part VII: Pleasant Interludes

Part VIII: Nice People

Part IX: Favorite Bird Stories

Appendix

PART I

THE BEGINNING

SHANGRI-LA

I grew up in a small town in North Dakota, where I learned that there is a big world out there.

Let's go back to 1928 to find a skinny, freckle-faced eight-year-old girl squinting through the heavy dust in the air, the sun only a small orange circle struggling to shed its rays to the ground. As she trudged along with a glass milk bottle and a nickel in her hands on her way to the grocery store to buy milk for the family, an errand she had performed many times, disaster struck! The returnable glass bottle, which was worth five cents, slipped out of her hands and burst into shards on the sidewalk. Sobbing, she returned to the downstairs apartment in the two-story duplex she shared with her mother, father, and younger sister. What if her mother did not have another nickel? Sometimes supper was only a bowl of milk mush topped with a crispy crust of sugar and cinnamon.

Every day that summer we watched for a cloud in the sky. Occasionally there were bolts of lightning and peals of thunder, but no rain came. Crops dried up and my father, one of the first farm insurance salesmen, suffered. If a few drops of rain fell, I ran outdoors and lifted my face to the sky. When lightning cracked open the sky, I tried to catch a glimpse of heaven, but the moment was too fleeting. All my life I have loved the crashes of a summer storm.

From the center of town I could see wheat fields in all directions. Each day three trains roared down the tracks after stopping at the roundhouse for water and fuel.

In the Dust Bowl years hobos rode the rails. Some of them, grimy and unkempt, jumped off the box cars and appeared at our back door begging for food. No matter how little we had, my mother always gave them a plateful of something hot. That happened quite often; we heard that the hobos made Xs, or some kind of a mark, in front of houses where they had found kindness. That was the rumor, anyway.

During the hot summer days, my sister and I spent hours in the unsupervised playground behind the newspaper office, swinging, bouncing on the teeter-totter and sliding down two curved steel rails as slippery as Greased Lightning. After a kind local philanthropist donated a small swimming pool to the town, we swam. Or played tennis on the two public clay courts.

But winter was wonderful, walking through softly falling snow to the river, where we joined the other boys and girls and skated against the wind as far as we wished, then flew back, the wind at our backs, to the open fire the bigger boys kept aflame. Never mind that I wore boy's black skates; I soared down the icy riverbank, jumped over the gaping space below, and landed on the ice as neatly as a butterfly on a leaf—over and over again. On the way home, I walked with my skates hanging over my shoulders. Under the winter moon the snow sparkled like a million diamonds.

Our town had four clothing stores: Montgomery Ward and

Penney's for everyday things and a women's apparel and men's clothing store for better dresses and suits. My school clothes were made by the local sewing lady, who also remodeled my mother's few outfits each fall. At last, in high school, I purchased a dress at Montgomery Ward—a black sheath with a white satin Peter Pan collar. I remember how proud I was to wear it.

My best friend's father owned the drugstore on the corner of Sixth and Main, and every week the magazine agent came in with the new editions, tore the covers off *True Story,* and threw the old issues into a discard pile, where Betty filched a copy for each of her friends. Therewith I learned about "life," especially unwanted pregnancies.

That eight-year-old girl had already read most of the books in the children's wing of the public library, the most wonderful place in town, where absolute silence was maintained by the gray-haired librarian. Joseph Altsheller was my favorite author. A tomboy at heart, I loved the stories about Indian boys and pioneers stealing silently through the forests on moccasined feet. But *Little Lucia's Lively Doings* frequently found its way home with me. Then came *Little Women* and its sequels (*Jo's Boys* was my favorite), Mark Twain, and Dickens. The adult section, located mainly behind the librarian's desk, finally lured me into tiptoeing around, closing my eyes, picking a book from the shelf, and reading whatever fell into my hands. That included all three segments of *The Forsythe Saga* and a green-covered book titled *Sand House,* my first encounter with naked sex in a novel.

I dreamed of Richard Halliburton's Shangri-la, the Tibet where he lost his life; and the Taj Mahal, which had been built to commemorate the memory of a dead wife; and who wouldn't be fascinated with a mountain named Kilimanjaro? At school, elbows on my desk, chin in my palms, I gazed out the windows as I tried to picture the fascinating places I had read about.

My mother had a problem with my love of books, which was that most of the time I spent indoors I spent reading. I didn't hear anything. Finally, in exasperation, she would grab the book and shout, "Harriet, I have been talking to you!"

My mother was determined that her daughters would go to college, so she began a study program in vocal music and graduated ready to teach. For many years, departing early and returning late, carrying a lunch box, she traveled by bus or train to three nearby small towns. On Mondays she rode the bus to another small town, a thirty-mile trip, to direct a church choir that annually offered an oratorio, a large community attraction. Every penny she earned was saved for our college education. Clara, a soft-spoken farm girl, came to live with us and attend high school. We girls were pretty much on our own.

My dad owned a small car, a Whippet. I had watched him depress the clutch and pull down the gearshift, and it seemed so easy. One summer day when I was ten, the car was parked on the street in front of our house and I decided to try driving. I turned the key, smoothly started off down the street, and then panicked as I saw the stop sign ahead of me in front of the post office on Main Street. I didn't know how to stop! I turned the wheels sharply and bumped over the curb, where a tree on our neighbor's perfectly manicured front lawn stopped me. Someone at the car dealership across the street must have phoned my dad, because within minutes he came running from his office, I suppose half-expecting to find a dead daughter. Suddenly, curious neighbors encircled the unharmed vehicle and an extremely embarrassed driver.

After that episode my dad took me on his evening drives to inspect farm buildings and allowed me to drive around the open farmyards to my heart's content. He taught me how to drive on muddy roads and on ice. Then one late afternoon when I was twelve, the phone rang and my mother picked it up to hear my dad say, "I am stuck in Moorhead with no way to get home. Send Harriet to pick me up at the Metropole Hotel."

Sitting straight as a ramrod and staring unwaveringly at the loosely graveled road ahead, I drove the fifty miles to the streets of Fargo, the largest city in the state, crossed the bridge to Minnesota, made the tense turns in the city to the downtown rendezvous, and found my dad anxiously waiting. With a tremendous sigh of relief, I slid out from under the wheel and let my dad take over. He had trusted me and I'd done it!

Until radio came to our little world, the Federated Women's Clubs of America was the main opportunity for prairie women to continue their education. Those programs inspired my mother, who had little formal education, to become one of the most well-read women I've ever known. After radio arrived, we never missed *Twenty Questions* or the Saturday performance of the Metropolitan Opera, with its interviews and comments by Milton Cross.

Why am I recalling my childhood of so long ago? Not in any way to denigrate the small town that has since grown, modernized, attracted industry, and supported my friends who chose to live there all their lives. At the age of eighteen I climbed the steps on one of those noisy trains and headed for the University of Michigan in Ann Arbor, and never looked back.

In the summer of 1940 I sailed aboard the liner *Lurline* to Hawaii to marry my fiancé, who was stationed on the heavy cruiser the *Indianapolis*. After we both survived the Japanese attack on Pearl Harbor, we decided during our fifty-nine years together that life is to savor—every minute of it.

So we have touched the inlaid gems of the Taj Mahal; as campers across Tanzania we have climbed Mt. Meru under the snows of Kilimanjaro; and from their sturdy ponies, the sunburned, leathery faces of Tibetans have smiled down at me. I have overnighted on the Drakenberg of South Africa, flown over the Okovanga Delta in a small plane, helicoptered to the hidden interior of Mauritius Island, and swum in the hot waters of a cave in Iceland and in the cool blue depths of the Indian Ocean.

I am proud of the four children we raised.

I think the austere years of our first-generation Norwegian family makes me daily grateful for the richness of my life, thankful for parents who instilled in my sister and me a desire to do our best and to be aware of the needs of others.

Yes, there really is a big world out there!

ADVICE TO NEW BIRDERS

Every new birder should have a guru. I was lucky; I had two. Their names are Will Russell and Davis Finch. I remember them as tall, thin young men wearing blue denim work shirts with frayed collars. Before the days of the now-popular tours, they had advertised a three-week trip, titled Northeast Birding (NEB), to the islands off northeast Canada in October 1959.

The idea was intriguing and fairly inexpensive. The tour would begin in Bangor, Maine; travel up the coast; then visit Brier Island, New Brunswick, and Machias Seal Island; and finish at the end of the season with a week on Monhegan Island, off the coast of Maine.

So my husband, Bill, and I collected back issues of *American Birds,* fall season, and made a list of the birds ordinarily seen in that region. We mailed the list and received a return phone call from Davis. He assured us we would see most of our ten wanted birds. We signed on.

We were fortunate to begin with Will and Davis what

became a lifelong birding career. When I showed disappointment at not finding a bird I was looking for, Will advised me to be content with what was *there*. That is how I learned which bird species dwell together. He taught me to be patient, which is probably why I never minded the long, quiet watches at the edge of a marsh, or sitting on a log in the forest until quiet resumed and the birds returned to their normal activities. That is how I found my first pileated woodpecker, which actually flew into a nest hole in the top of the tree I was sitting under in northern Michigan. Will taught me to study each species in detail in order to remember little things, such as the white lacy edges on the wings of the immature royal tern we were studying through scopes on the beach at Cape May one autumn.

Early on, Davis taught me to be certain of my identification. I remember on an overnight stay on Machias Seal Island we encountered a captive flock of fall warblers. After dinner, as we sat around a low table in the lounge of the little hotel compiling a trip list of the species we had seen that day, I named a warbler that immediately caught the attention of our guides. Instead of saying, "I don't believe you," Davis suggested that we find it again. The two of us went out and relocated the warbler flock, but, of course, there was no Davidson warbler. I had named a species that had never been recorded there. Years later I stood beside Davis for an hour or more on a cold morning on Attu Island, memorizing the shape of the no-bill (well, almost) marbled murrelet. Patience, patience.

Six participants signed up for that first NEB tour. Will and Davis had rented two station wagons, each of them driving, and we proceeded from the pine-forested coast to the islands, crossing on ferry boats. We did a fair amount of hiking, but I will never forget the day on Brier Island, in the midst of a rainstorm and furiously blowing winds, when backed up against the shelter of a lighthouse, we sighted our first manx shearwaters beating against the wind. Nor will I forget the day we went to sea in a small fishing boat and encountered pairs of humpback whales surfing together. As we watched their breaching in fascination, one whale surfaced under our boat; we could have touched it. As we all certainly expected to be tipped into the icy waters, the mighty leviathan slowly sank under the waves.

In the following years we followed our gurus to many states on NEB weekends—Florida, Arizona, Texas, Colorado, New Jersey, Minnesota—and I vow we never missed a day of birding because of the weather. And that is where I learned the term "tertials." (I love that word even though I sometimes forget to look for them, or cannot find them.)

I wonder if on that first Canadian Island tour we began to have an inkling that a life of adventure lay ahead of us. "Life list" wasn't even in our vocabulary back then. Right there we had added ten species to our short life list. But the lessons we learned from Will and Davis made it possible for us to go birding by ourselves into many corners of the world. We compiled our target lists, studied the habitats, and found transportation—from flying on jets to faraway continents, to curling up behind Jerry Stensel in the small space of his Piper Cub on our way to camping in the Brooks Range. We found ourselves diving through a small hole in a cloud to land a six-seater Dornier on the sand spit of St. Lawrence Island in the Bering Sea, or slowly drifting down onto the grassy meadows of the Fiji Islands.

Will and Davis built their birding skills into a successful tour company. I take some credit for helping them get started. And I have taken their advice. Now I am the expert! I am the one who says, "There it is!"

PART II

BIRD CHASES

IN SEARCH OF THE ROSS'S GULL

March 1974

It began when a friend mailed us a clipping from the *New York Times* describing the sighting of a rare arctic Ross's gull in an estuary on the Atlantic coast at Salisbury, Massachusetts. Our ornithologist friend Davis Finch had commented, "This has got to be the bird of the century!" and we could almost hear him add, "Gosh, this is really unbelievable." Then local friends stopped us on the street and asked, "Did you see the NBC special on that rare bird?" (We had missed it.) Then *Time* magazine ran the story on page one.

After discussing the unprecedented event at dinner one night, we suddenly found ourselves planning an expedition to the East Coast to look for the gull. A fast route from Michigan involved driving across Canada to Niagara Falls and the New York Freeway. The next morning my husband wrapped up office business for a long weekend while I assembled a three-day supply of sandwiches, fruit, and snacks; a one-burner backpack stove; a coffee pot; and thermoses filled with hot coffee, tea, and bouillon. We packed a change of clothing and threw sleeping bags and foam mattresses in the station wagon. By midafternoon we began driving.

It was my turn to drive from midnight until three o'clock in the morning while my husband slept through the midnight traffic. Only giant semis rumbled past me on the dark mountain passes of New York and Massachusetts—comforting companions of the night. Then it was my turn to sleep, and when I awoke we were in Salisbury at dawn, driving on unfamiliar streets and beginning our search for the Ross's gull.

First we learned a lesson in local geography—Salisbury lies on the north side of the estuary of the Merrimac River, and Newburyport lies on the south. Each side had vantage points from which observers could look over the channel, but the famous wall where news cameramen had focused on hundreds of birders with binoculars and telescopes was on the Newburyport side. There, all newcomers congregated to gather the latest information. There, one could find anywhere from a dozen to several hundred shivering spectators while the tide was either ebbing or flowing.

We were the second arrivals that Friday morning, so we joined a young couple already scanning the gulls on mudflats below the dike for a Ross's. The group grew to two dozen until at high tide, when the last gull had disappeared to its resting place, we dispersed to explore other observation points.

We found the inlet to the estuary, where ocean waves crashed against a rock break wall, sending spume a hundred feet into the air. We found a path to the beach on the Salisbury side. Salisbury State Beach offered a different view over another section of the estuary. But nowhere did we see a small gull with a wedge-shaped tail and red feet. By nightfall we gave up, dined in a restaurant that served delicious seafood, and were lucky to get a room in the only neighborhood motel. Would you believe that we had no trouble falling asleep?

During the night the predicted snowstorm arrived. We awoke to gale force winds and swirling white flakes, not an auspicious beginning for a day of seabird watching. Now we indeed needed the down vests, snowmobile suits, boots, wool caps, and long raincoats to keep us dry for the next twelve hours outdoors.

Saturday brought hordes of weekend birders and many expert eyes. But again the observation wall was not productive. By ten o'clock groups broke up to search in other places. We drove around to the state beach, disconsolately eyeing flocks of snow buntings and Lapland longspurs, ordinarily cheery little fellows, but not now. Seeing cars assembling at the tumultuous inlet, we joined the crowd. Suddenly a young man came running and breathlessly calling, "They have the bird—follow me!" Encumbered with scopes, binoculars, and cameras, everybody ran for vehicles and screeched along the country road, and in five minutes arrived at a group excitedly looking through scopes and shouting directions.

But we were too late—already the little gull had departed. This time, however, we could follow its flight by driving another five minutes to the Salisbury side, where another group of searchers had the rare bird in sight and we had a glimpse of a tiny bird bobbing in the water, far away but with noticeably long wings tilted upward. It was not a very satisfactory identification, but we could say we had seen it. Within a minute it disappeared and the tide was high.

We sighed. For several hours we and our companions waited until the ebbing of the tide stirred the gull colony to feeding activity again, but the birds swirled up and away en masse and so swiftly that we grudgingly abandoned our watch to return to the wall in Newburyport, where it was now freezing cold but windless and bathed in sunshine.

Within minutes after our arrival we heard the shout, "There he is!" followed by a string of confusing directions: "He's flying right!"

"In front of the red buoy!" "Now he's up!" "Now he's down!" "Coming toward us!" At last we picked up the Ross's gull in flight, watched it bank and flash its wedged tail, saw the unmarked light gray wings, and occasionally in the late afternoon sunshine, the faint pink wash on the breast. The bird chose to settle down to feed in the far distance, but now we felt we really had experienced one of the rarest bird sightings in recent birding history.

Was a bird in flight enough? Not for us. We would give it another try Sunday morning. An even larger throng of determined weekend birders was at the wall as the morning low tide began to rise; this time the shout "There he is!" guided our gaze to the little Ross's gull feeding on the mudflats in front of us—preening, fluttering before our eyes, showing us even his bright red feet. Now we were satisfied.

The Ross's gull was not the only rare bird wintering on the estuary. At periods of high tide each day we had several hours to look for other European wanderers to our shores. We found a very uncommon visitor in the tufted duck from northern Europe, which resembles its associate, our scaup, except for his all-dark back and a distinctive waving plume at the back of his head. Several all-white Iceland gulls were casual visitors from their native country. And we noted our old friend the European black-headed gull, though now in winter plumage he had only a spot of black behind his eye. Several little gulls from southern Europe appeared in the flocks every day—the smallest gull of all.

Did you think a seagull is a seagull? There is no such thing! In addition to those I have just mentioned, herring, ringbills, and Bonaparte's gulls surrounded us.

We started the long trip home. Tired? Yes, but no other bleak, gray March had offered us such a bright ending.

A SEARCH FOR THE RARE SPOTTED OWL
May 1975

"Spotted Owl: Uncommon permanent resident of dense coniferous forest. Usually roosts in thick clumps of second-growth pine. Your chances of finding this bird are not good. When its particular call is heard it is so distinctive that it cannot be forgotten; however, this call is not often heard."

—James A. Lane, author of
A Birder's Guide to Southern California and
Finding Birds in Southeastern Arizona

It is our habit when vacationing in an area new to us to make a list of all the birds that might be found there and deliberately search for them—a game we have played now for many years. But never before had we felt confident enough to try to locate those creatures of the night world, the owls. We had read about the spotted owl, this large dark brown forest owl with its puffy round head, large dark eyes, and heavily spotted underparts that inhabits heavy forests in wooded canyons, but we were not daunted by the information about its forbidding habitat. We made a tape recording of its call from a record of western bird songs before starting out on a birding trip to Arizona and southern California.

Then one night, while guests of my cousin in Big Bear Lake, California, we timidly crept into the back row of the Big Bear

Lake Historical Society meeting at the local junior high school because the Big Bear Lake weekly newspaper had advertised a slide presentation, "Birds of the San Bernardino Mountains," by the curator of the San Bernardino County Museum.

Dr. Eugene Cardiff was not only an entertaining lecturer, but an avid practical ornithologist who actually spent a good deal of time taking students on field trips in that area. But we could not take our eyes off the display on the table in the front of the room: two beautiful stuffed dark brown spotted owls.

After the program was over, we crowded near Dr. Cardiff and asked so many questions that he almost missed the Kool-Aid and cookies. He described a densely forested mountain road near the Hannah Flats campground where he thought a spotted owl had been heard, and he enthusiastically encouraged us to try to find it.

So the next night at dusk, with my cousin driving us, we proceeded up the narrow, curving road to the campground; waited for darkness; then walked around, repeatedly playing our tape recording and intently listening for an answering call. Dark shapes of tall ponderosa pines swayed against the first-quarter moon. Not discouraged by failure, we drove along the deeply rutted road, stopping regularly to try our luck.

At an altitude of seven thousand feet, the night air blew cold and nearly froze our fingers. Lights from the valley twinkled far below. Once, we heard the repetitious note of the pygmy owl in the distance, and occasionally the hoot of the great horned owl. Our expert driver was not happy about maneuvering along the poorly maintained rock-strewn trail. Eventually we admitted defeat, drank hot chocolate from the thermos for warmth, and headed for home at nearly midnight.

Two days later we were driving a few miles higher in the mountains when we noticed several stands of extremely dense pine trees. Simultaneously my husband and I exclaimed, "Let's try here for the spotted owl!"

Again the three of us ate an early dinner and started up the mountain in the fading evening light. We carefully followed the twisting, turning road to its highest point, then at quarter-mile intervals descended from the car and played the taped calls into the black outlines of pines. No answer. Again and again we thought we had found a suitable habitat. The dense forest seemed impenetrable.

Doggedly we repeated the procedure, five minutes at each stop. Suddenly my husband felt rather than saw a moving shape. "There he is!" he whispered, and we flashed our bright beacons on a big beautiful dark brown owl staring at us from a pine branch! How long he gazed at us I do not know, but at last he began a penetrating wild cry that I knew I wanted to preserve. I dashed to the car and grabbed a blank tape, clipped it into place with shaking fingers, and returned to catch the last four ghostly shrieks before the owl lifted its enormous wings and softly and silently glided away. Again it called to us from a distant height; then we heard it no more.

Excited, hysterically hilarious conversation on the way down the mountain betrayed our elation at the success of our adventure. The owl was so big and so splendid. In the mountain world, far above mortals' dwellings, we had been privileged, for a few seconds, to pierce the secret hiding place of one of nature's rare creatures. I shall preserve that bit of tape, with its wild notes, to forever recall that night already etched so deeply in my memory.

You were right, Jim Lane.

A EUROPEAN VISITOR

March 1976

Do you remember the big ice storm of March 2, 1976, the one that clothed the world in fragile, crystalline beauty, but whose force destroyed power lines and brought disaster to Michigan communities for days? That was the day my husband decided he could get away from his law office long enough to go searching with me for a robin-sized North European thrush, a fieldfare, that somehow had flown off course and found its way into woods near a small Quebec village near Montreal and had kept itself alive by feeding in apple trees in the yard of a small country home.

The fieldfare had been identified around Christmastime. A friend of ours had seen the bird in the middle of February and given us explicit directions to the site. It would be a long drive with no guarantee that we would find the bird. We also imagined the homeowner irate as dozens of strangers with binoculars invaded his yard on weekends.

As winter temperatures soared into the fifties and sixties in the last days of February, just before the March storm, spring fever struck. Daily I brought up the subject of the fieldfare. Once I even suggested that we drive all night and arrive in the village of Rigaud at dawn.

The morning we awoke to an ice-covered world, my husband announced that the next day he had a morning meeting, but afterward would be free to take me to search for the fieldfare. Oh happy day!

Canada's highway map indicated that we would have expressway driving all the way. Nothing extra to pack except food for a two-day trip. I pushed out of my mind weather reports of "rain," "freezing drizzle," and "driver's advisory," but I did take the precaution of tossing in a raincoat and snowsuit on top of a sleeping bag and wool blankets in case of a nighttime driving emergency.

Rain still misted down as we crossed the bridge to Canada shortly before noon. We settled down to the monotonous sweep of windshield wipers, driving in shifts until evening when the chill of night suddenly froze wet pavement into the worst of driving dangers—sheet ice. Our ordinarily stable station wagon fishtailed. Truckers convoyed, driving their giant vehicles in the center of the two lanes, and only grudgingly moved over just enough to let us pass. We were exhausted and relieved when we pulled into the small dark town of Rigaud after midnight, hoping we would find a motel. We did, and we slept.

We were up again before dawn. Instant oatmeal not only is a practical invention, but tastes delicious when one is eager to be off on an adventure. I pulled a snowsuit over my wool slacks and ragg wool sweater. White snow still covered the province of Quebec. Two days of freezing rain had glazed the countryside into fields of shining ice. However, our mile drive to the house in early daylight was not difficult. Mr. Howard, who had become the self-appointed director of this unusual bird sanctuary, welcomed us. He indicated a narrow space between his garage and house and pointed to an already worn pathway to a small white outbuilding, from the corner of which one was mostly likely to view the fieldfare as it approached its favorite apple tree.

We stood at the edge of several acres of woods, which extended as far as a distant railroad track, with another grove beyond. Birds already were flitting to the backyard feeders—chickadees; redpolls; titmice; and noisy gold, black, and white evening grosbeaks. Could we find one small thrush among all those trees and amid all those fluttering creatures? We had food and coffee. We prepared ourselves to stay all day.

The ice-covered twigs began to melt, dripping onto the icy ground with a delicate tinkle. We stationed ourselves at different corners of the shed. A black squirrel entertained us as it scampered through the trees. Soon we were joined by three young men who had driven all night cramped into a Volkswagen! They tried to tiptoe quietly toward us, but in vain—their big boots crashed and crackled through the hard snow crust.

Time dissolved. I was watching the apple trees near the house, thinking hopelessly that if our target bird did fly in, I wouldn't be able to see it through the dense tangle of branches, when a thrush that wasn't a robin alighted on a low, clearly visible branch. Even before I raised my binoculars I sensed it was the fieldfare—he had a pale gray head and a rusty yellow breast streaked with black, and he was looking directly at me. It took two seconds to confirm and in a low voice announce my find to my husband and the boys, who were only a few steps away.

The famous bird did not hurry away. When he finally did fly, we picked him up again with binoculars as he flew into a nearby tree, where he turned one way, then another, until we had all had a fine view of his markings. Then he flew away across the tracks and into the distant woods. I looked at my watch. It was only eight o'clock in the morning!

We wished the boys luck; they were on their way to search for another rare European wanderer, the smew, still being seen on a pond in Newport, Rhode Island. We headed for home and into an impenetrably dense fog that blanketed our highway for the next four hours. To make matters worse, rain began to pour down. In fact, the tense driving became so unbearable that we stopped at a rest area and, safe inside our warm station wagon, ate our picnic lunch.

Not until we neared Toronto in the late afternoon did the skies clear, and then suddenly! Completely! It was as if we had shot from the underworld into heaven! The sun on white cloud formations blinded our eyes as we proceeded west to Lake Huron and home.

It was an exhilarating conclusion to our adventure. From doubt and danger we had emerged into victory and elation. Two happy people drove along, silently saying thank you for our safe return.

TWO FOR THE PRICE OF ONE

May 1977

The Elusive Cuckoo

Cuckoos are slim, long-tailed, sinuous-looking birds, a little longer than a robin, olive-brown above and white below. The rare mangrove cuckoo has yellowish-buff underparts and a black mask that extends behind the eyes. And he lives in mangrove swamps, which elicit frightening images of alligators, snakes, and witch doctors. In reality, the mangrove world is filled with graceful herons, stately roseate spoonbills, and golden-slippered snowy egrets.

For several days we had patrolled the mangrove-bordered roads of Sugarloaf Key, Florida, without catching sight or sound of a mangrove cuckoo, a most desirable addition to our life list of North American birds. Mid-May is the optimal place and time to discover one as the birds return from their southern wintering grounds.

One day, when rain thwarted our plans to go fishing in the Gulf Stream, we decided to return to Sugarloaf Key for one more try. With travel trailer in tow, on our way we stopped to choose a campsite at Bahia Honda State Park just as the rain swept in a torrent over the Florida Keys in a midafternoon flood. Within minutes campers' tents were floating in two feet of rushing water. Never before had we experienced eleven inches of rain in a single storm! There was frightful devastation around us. Campers struggled to save their belongings, which were floating away in a muddy, raging current. The water surging around us almost reached the highest step of our trailer.

Half an hour later the storm subsided, clouds hung low, and still rain-jacketed we emerged from the safety of our trailer, slogged the short distance to our station wagon, and decided to revisit Sugarloaf Key in the early evening. In the momentary lulls between showers, we trudged down the tree-canopied narrow dirt road, and at the same time scrutinized every tangled section of twisted roots for a foraging bird shape.

My husband, ranging ahead of me, suddenly gave a whistle, which sent me speeding toward him. He had flushed a mangrove cuckoo! There it was: long, white-spotted tail hanging down, strong decurved bill, and the telltale mask that looked as though someone had streaked the line with a paintbrush, recognizable even at dusk. A beer can lay on the path. Ordinarily we would have carried it out; instead, we left it there as a marker.

Rain poured down all night. It was a good morning for sleeping in, so, rather late for birders, we returned to Sugarloaf Key in midmorning in an attempt to photograph the cuckoo. Three new birders arrived and decided to join us as we walked, looked, and listened along the stretch of trail on either side of the beer can. Then the bird called. Crouched at the edge of the swamp, we waited. We could hear him in the treetops over our heads, foraging from one limb to another. Then he perched out in the open and it was time for photographs. A friendly, rare cuckoo.

We have made many drives up and down the Florida Keys, but this adventure was special!

The Bird That Gives Away His Hiding Place

While camping in Michigan, we have often fallen asleep to the monotonous calls of the whip-poor-will, endlessly repeating his name with a lilting accent on the last syllable. Occasionally we have flushed one during a walk in the woods, then followed his erratic flight to a tree limb, where he melted into the bark. In the South his counterpart is the chuck-will's-widow, a similar but larger and browner bird that inhabits pine woods and utters his name at dawn and at dusk.

In our efforts to identify a chuck-will's-widow over a period of several weeks during our Florida birding trip to the Everglades National Park, we had exhausted ourselves and our patience as we chased him with a spotlight after dark and again before dawn. Always he flew tantalizingly away and began calling from a new spot in the dark forest.

It was the last morning of our trip. Rain drenched the world as we drove out of Pinewoods Campground in total darkness at five-thirty in the morning. Chuck-will's-widows called from far away. But shortly before we reached the main road, we heard one call from fairly near us. We stopped. We looked at each other, neither one wanting to make the decision. Another failure? We decided to make one last try to find that bird.

My husband led the way. Then began one of the most bizarre chases of our birding careers. We precariously stumbled through the dripping undergrowth over a forest floor, built up through the centuries, of slimy, rotting logs and concealed ancient subterranean man traps. A misstep? Unthinkable! Neither moon nor stars silhouetted the ranks of the forest trees. Only our spotlight, which after what seemed hours finally reflected the eye of the calling bird. Then, as we neared, like all the other "chucks" before him, he fluttered away. We clutched at the frail support of thin saplings and slowly picked our way back to the road.

Then occurred one of those rare circumstances that happens to every explorer. We flushed our chuck-will's-widow, and this time he flew to a perch at the top of a tree stump directly in front of us! Our spotlight encircled his body, and our binoculars clearly revealed his brown feathers and pulsating throat as he continued his predawn song.

The ending was predictable. When I am in the field, I always wear high leather boots. That morning, as I laced my new white Pro-Keds, I had announced, "No way am I going into the woods this morning!"

HOW TO FIND A GREAT GRAY OWL

August 1977–May 1978

I read a lot about birds so that when we have time to look for a hard-to-find species we will have a reasonable chance of locating one. The great gray owl, a northern pine forest dweller and the largest owl in North America, became almost an illusion—he appeared on annual reports and on wildlife refuge checklists, but whenever we arrived, nobody seemed to know about him!

One hot August we set up camp at Lava Beds National Monument in northern California, where the park naturalist verified a report that the great gray owl occasionally appeared around Mammoth Crater, an enormous rock-rimmed gorge formed by violent volcanic eruptions hundreds of thousands of years ago. We immediately drove to the crater.

It was evening. We stumbled over the strewn lava at dusk, minding our footsteps more than looking up for a big bird. Again at dawn we completely circled the rim, even discovering another hidden crater lined with marvelous caves one might expect a wise old owl to claim for a nesting site. We spotted roosting ledges high above white droppings, which indicated a favorite perch for some kind of raptor. If careful scrutiny with binoculars could have exposed an owl shape, not even a tiny saw-whet owl would have escaped us.

But we did not give up that year. A few days later we talked to a refuge manager who had actually seen great gray owls perched along a country road bordering Upper Klamath Basin in southern Oregon. He told us to go to Mare's Egg Spring.

In the USDA Forest Service campground at Aspen Point, tucked in among the crowded, towering pine trees, the damp coolness contrasted dramatically with the shimmering heat of the lava beds we had recently visited. So we camped overnight, then went looking for the spring the next morning.

Our destination was almost as elusive as the owl, since we had had no previous experience with mare's eggs so didn't know what to look for to find Mare's Egg Spring. On the particular morning we had chosen, the Pacific Northwest was engulfed in drenching rain, extremely welcome in the mountain areas where recent fires had already decimated thousands of acres of forest but unfortunate for two rather sleepy birders walking along at dawn.

Mare's eggs (we had stopped to study a helpful roadside plaque) are algae that stick together in gelatinous balls and come in all sizes, from pinheads to baseballs. We didn't see any in the spring, and three hours of searching trees and stumps along the logging trails failed to produce a great gray owl, either. Water from our rain hoods dripped on our eyelashes and binoculars. As a parting gesture, my husband imitated the low-pitched hoot of the great gray. Out of the dim forest came one answering "Whoo-oo," then silence. In vain we tried to coax out another sound. He was there, all right, but not for man to see, so we left the great gray to his wilderness solitude.

Then we heard from a reliable California birder that sighting a great gray owl was a certainty in Yosemite National Park. We had only to drive to Crane Flat Campground and the owl would be sitting on a stump waiting for us. Our station wagon and travel trailer labored slowly up the tortuously curved road in the pine forest of one of our most beautiful national recreation areas, strangely quiet in late September long after the hordes of summer vacationers had departed.

The first indication of trouble ahead came when we learned that the Crane Flat Campground was closed! The nearest alternative was a primitive site only three miles farther on. If we had known the difficulty of inching our way down, in and out among the rocks and trees on the narrowest of roads, hugging the inside curves where the trail edge skirted deep chasms, crawling around hairpin turns, we would never have witnessed a campsite of such grandeur that the tremendous gray boulders, which in some ancient era had somehow tumbled into their permanent positions here, dwarfed our manmade vehicle.

For three days we monitored the well-known great gray owl stakeout from before dawn until after dark. The naturalists in the park office assured us that the owls commonly foraged over the area or surveyed park traffic from one of the many wooden fence posts alongside the highway. We expected the silent shadow of gray wings at any moment. But our holiday time ended, and we were forced to leave the park and start for home, sadly and slowly working our way out from the strangest and grandest camp home we had ever known.

The next spring, in mid-May, we heard about a possible nesting site for great gray owls in northern Minnesota near the Canadian border. A few days later our travel trailer was parked in a small-town campground while we examined every pine tree bordering every open area along the county roads. Most owls are best spotted at dawn or dusk, but great grays also perch brazenly right in the middle of the day, so the birding hours stretched from early mornings to late evenings, until I was too tired to get up in the predawn darkness again.

It was a Sunday morning. My husband quietly slipped out of our camper, and I knew he was going to try again for the owl, but I snuggled deeper into my sleeping bag and quickly fell asleep again. The next words I heard were not in a dream; my husband was shaking me and half-shouting, "I saw the great gray owl!"

In a very few minutes I was dressed and we were on our way back to the county road where we had patrolled so often before—back to the telephone pole from which the owl had flown such a short time earlier. He wasn't there!

We searched and searched until bright daylight surrounded us. I wanted to cry with disappointment, yet I knew I had only myself to blame. At last, in a final effort, we parked our car and walked slowly along the narrow shoulder of the road, and then, miracle of miracles, the owl was sitting in a meadow on the opposite side of the water-filled roadside ditch!

His two-foot height blended into the previous year's brown grass like a weathered tree stump. Black lines etched concentric circles on the huge facial discs that surrounded yellow eyes. White tufts under his chin resembled a neat bow tie. Fearlessly and majestically he stared at his approaching visitors, then turned his attention, with the piercing eyes of a wild hunter, to the task of searching for food. He was truly king of the northern forest and bog.

We lingered, absorbing details of the dark streakings on the gray feathers, the forward tilt of the motionless body, the surrounding camouflage of gray tree trunks, and the still-leafless branches of saplings and bush. Then slowly the great gray spread his mighty wings, silently glided across the little meadow, and disappeared among the dense pines.

Here in his unconfining home territory, untouched and rarely visited by man, we sensed the strength and beauty of one of our country's most magnificent creatures. The long search was over. I will remember the unexpected encounter with Mr. Great Gray as a very special spring morning.

A TINY JEWEL IN THE BIRD KINGDOM

May 1978

I stood there, rain dripping from my raincoat like big tears, apropos of my dark thoughts on the subject of California weather in January. The South Coast Botanic Garden is the home of the tiny Allen's hummingbird. In my dreams, this sanctuary on the Palos Verdes Peninsula jutting into the Pacific Ocean had radiated warmth, fragrance, and beauty. On the contrary, my hands dug into my pockets for comfort, a plastic bag protected my binoculars from ruin, and only the park naturalist's comment that "hummingbirds have to eat, you know, even in the rain" drew us back to our determined vigil in the late afternoon.

Even the large Rivoli's hummingbird is only five inches long. Middle-sized hummers, such as the common Anna's, average three and a half to three and three-quarters inches. But the Allen's is only three inches! Both Anna's and Allen's have green backs and red throats, but Anna's has a red forehead and green tail, while Allen's has a green cap and a rufous tail. Which is all very clear when one studies a field guide, but hummers are not noted for posing for portraits.

We sighed, occasionally shuffled back and forth near the green shrubbery, and stared as if our very desire could magnetize the tiny bird to appear. But the rain never ceased and darkness fell.

The following morning mere mist enveloped the gardens as we hurried down the path to the aloes. Aloes? We thought they were the green shrubs surrounded by orange cone-shaped flowers on stalks as tall as my waist. Fortunately, a gardener, covered in a yellow rain poncho and dragging a forked tool, stopped by for conversation. The aloes, he explained, are the bright blossoms planted in patches among the rocks, and hummingbirds love them.

The new information and fairly good morning light predicted imminent success in our search. During the next hour our excitement intensified. The first hummingbird to show up for breakfast was a male Costa's, who peered down on us from a perch in a small tree; perhaps insulted by our lack of interest, he flew away. Then several Anna's erratically flashed by on their private pathways.

After that, nothing. A half hour passed, during which several Anna's hummingbirds darted, hovered, and hummed around the aloe patches, one whirring in midair at my shoulder, the morning light eliciting brilliant iridescence on its head and throat. My mind wandered to the possibility of catching a hummingbird with a butterfly net. The recollection of the many July mornings at Wisconsin Audubon Camp, where bright orange-and-black monarch butterflies had easily eluded my clumsy grabs, and a glance down at my thick-soled boots brought into focus a picture of me facedown in the mud, and the idea faded.

My husband stood stolidly, feet apart, also scanning the aloe patch. For two hours we had waited patiently, when he softly called, "Here it is!" Quickly I moved to his side, and I, too, saw the tiny hummingbird, feeding up one side, down the other, then round and round the orange raceme. A few minutes later another lovely, colorful Allen's hummingbird darted out of the shrubby backdrop to dine daintily on the same blossom.

We had driven out of our way to find this distinctly local bird species. I started for the gate, hesitating only once to study a water pipit pecking on the sanctuary lawn. By the time my husband caught up with me, the rain was again pouring down in sheets.

Not a good day for watching birds!

BALTIMORE CANYON CHRISTMAS COUNT

December 1978

Northern gannet, dovekie, razorbill auk, black-legged kittiwake, great skua, great black-backed gull, red-throated loon, Bonaparte's gull, double-crested cormorant, horned grebe, snow goose, white-winged scoter, bald eagle, Carolina chickadee. An unusual Christmas count for Michiganders on a freezing December thirtieth!

The year before, we had the good fortune to participate in the Bodega Bay, California, offshore Christmas count and identified ancient murrelets and Thayer's gulls amid all the other alcids, gulls, and sea ducks on a typical winter's day off the Pacific shore. Strange that this year's highlight for us should be another pelagic trip, this time off the Atlantic coast on the first Baltimore Canyon Christmas count out of Ocean City, Maryland. (Audubon Society members all over the nation count birds seen on one specific day the week before or after Christmas.)

Over the past few winters we had appeared three times at six o'clock in the morning in appropriate apparel at different points along the Eastern Seaboard only to have our trips scrapped because of stormy weather. For this Christmas count we had made our reservation months before, but now the reality of sailing to sea on a midwinter's day presented the problems of our needing to have warm clothing and food. We would be on deck from six o'clock in the morning until six o'clock in the evening. We knew the ocean could be extremely rough, and we needed to protect ourselves from wind and ocean spray. We were out to find dovekies, a razorbill auk, and a great skua, but ocean birds make no promises or appointments.

The five-thirty boarding was in complete darkness; shadowy figures in down jackets, rubber boots, and all kinds of foul-weather gear jostled into the small fishing boat cabin, dumping backpacks and lunch boxes in corners and hurrying on deck for the departure, when the boat would ease into the harbor as dawn tinged the sky with enough light to see the outlines of birds flying over the break wall. As the light grew brighter, we watched the flight of large black-backed gulls, herring gulls, and dainty Bonaparte's gulls. Then the captain started the fifty-mile run to Baltimore Canyon, a huge cleavage in the continental shelf where upwellings bring nutrients to the surface and attract fish, which in turn attract seabirds.

Our prayers were answered. The ocean mirrored the sky in its calmness; birds swarmed in flocks close to the surface of the water. Gannets and black-legged kittiwakes became "trash birds." Then came the dovekies, tiny black-and-white alcids, which continued to pass by until the total count for the day grew to an unprecedented 279! Statistics from previous pelagic trips at this time of year had prepared us for a fleeting glimpse of three or four, if we were lucky. What a Christmas present!

For hours we monitored the bow and stern alternately; then the great skuas came—six in all throughout the day, big brown bull-necked pirates with white wing patches.

By midafternoon our boat began its return journey, and we sadly resigned ourselves to the fact that we would not secure a razorbill for the day's trophy. We had given up all hope when, from his lookout position in the bow, Chandler Robbins called out, "Big alcid in a flock of dovekies at twelve o'clock!"

Looking down on the fleet of birds in the water, we had no doubt that we had our razorbill, and a most cooperative one. He floated in the water at the bow of our boat, rode the swells, and posed for photographs, silhouetting the shape of his laterally compressed bill.

For us it was a triumph, the end of a long search that had led us to braving subzero days along the rocky coast, midnight arrivals in winter, and predawn disappointments when our ships failed to sail.

Old birders never die; they just sign on for another pelagic trip, which we immediately did. What did we expect to find? Cory's shearwaters in the summertime. Where? Off Ocean City, Maryland, of course!

THE KEY WEST QUAIL DOVE BIRD CHASE

February 1979

I have just returned from the South, but not from a peaceful vacation soaking up sun on the beach. I have completed my first solo bird chase—for a Key West quail dove, which was sighted in Everglades National Park in Florida; even in its natural range in the Bahamas it is a rare sighting on most of the islands.

Having heard about the dove, the decision to go look for it plagued me for a week until the impulsive moment when I phoned for a reservation on a night flight from Detroit to Fort Lauderdale. A few hours later I was on my way to the airport, my only luggage a carry-on bag, binoculars, and a telescope. I knew I was taking a chance. The dove had been there for three weeks already.

My friends Jake and Lillian Smith buzzed me through their apartment security gate at three-thirty in the morning, and with my alarm clock set for five-thirty I slept soundly for two hours. At six Jake handed me a cup of steaming black coffee and the keys to his car, and I took off on a secondary mission, keeping a promise I had made to myself that if I were ever in Florida in the spring I would try to find the masked duck that annually lurks in the far southeast corner of the last fenced pond at Loxahatchee Wildlife Refuge.

From my many visits there, the route was familiar. I turned in at the Loxahatchee signpost, passed the ranger's office on my right and the flooded marsh on my left, parked at the dike, and began walking rapidly toward the last lagoon, more than a mile away. My flashlight pierced the blackness of the sanctuary; rustlings and a few eerie calls assured me that I had company nearby. Eventually silvery pink flushed the eastern sky, and big and little dark shapes flitted among the reeds, sensing the arrival of a new day. The predawn curtain of shadows suddenly lifted, and just inside the chain-link fence ducks, coots, and gallinules like wooden decoys rocked silently.

The masked duck, which had eluded me over the years on many other morning visits, was there—in the center of the fleet, turning, turning, slowly turning. Then, as bright daylight flooded the refuge, he vanished among the reeds, where I knew he would so successfully blend into his surroundings that daytime observers could look directly at him and never see his shape.

Now I was ready for the serious search for the dove. Convincing Lillian that to go walking in the Everglades would be a glorious experience was not easy, but shortly after eight o'clock we drove the two-and-a-half-hour turnpike route deep into the Everglades National Park to Snake Bight Trail, where already a dozen cars, vans, and campers were parked. "Lucky us," thought I, knowing from experience that birders coming out from a sighting would pass along information and even point out the location of the bird. It would be large, iridescent above and white underneath, and distinguished by a noticeable white stripe below the eye.

Almost immediately we met a man who had seen the quail dove in late afternoon the day before. "It hasn't been seen yet today," he said, "but don't bother to go farther than a road to the left, about half a mile in." So we poked along, peering into the underbrush on either side of the path, startled by the croak of a green-backed heron, fascinated by the elegant stance of a great egret. We encountered other birders from faraway places: New York, Massachusetts, Connecticut, and Tennessee. A Los Angeles doctor had come straight from the hospital and flown through the night, and had presently gone without sleep for thirty-six hours. A young couple pushed a four-month-old baby girl named Julia in a canvas stroller. Snuggled in a yellow bunting, she slept peacefully.

By midafternoon, as mosquito pests increased their activity, Lillian politely refrained from reminding me that I had promised a lovely outing. I had to admit that for a nonbirder she more than proved our deep friendship; she never stopped searching, all the while slapping at the pesky insects that were attacking the damp hair under her golf visor.

Observers extended the search range another mile. An amateur photographer who had seen the bird the day before returned with his camera. He had marked the spot near a strangler fig, which I learned was a tree that began life by sending down strands of rootlets that, upon reaching the ground, began to grow. Eventually the rootlets strangle their host and grow into a full-sized fig tree. The tree demonstrates in its fantastically intertwined sculpture another of nature's infinite variety of forms.

Someone asked if the dove made any sounds. The Los Angeles doctor offered, "It has a very loud call: *Kee-ee-west! Kee-ee-west!*" Just as my tired brain was registering this interesting fact, he apologized for the frivolous concoction born of sleeplessness and frustration.

As dusk approached, observers departed one by one until we, too, gave up. We drove north in darkness.

Too soon it was five-thirty in the morning again. Alone, I drove back to the Snake Bight Trail, now in a rented car. Already vehicles of all sizes and shapes lined the shoulder of the highway. Surely the birders had discovered the dove! The young couple and baby Julia were there. Also the Los Angeles doctor and several other familiar faces.

All day our band of birders patrolled the trail, some brave young ones even penetrating into the parallel jungle habitat. At noon the doctor had to leave to catch his plane. The young couple with the baby departed to their campground. As the day's shadows lengthened, I dragged an enormous brown palm frond onto the path in front of the strangler fig, my sole clue to the dove's last sighting and disappearance. I could not have felt more dejected, driving away in the dark.

I almost did not return the next morning, a Monday. I gulped down Jake's hot coffee, said good-bye to my friends, who had been supportive hosts, and drove the long trip back to the southern tip of the Everglades. It was nine o'clock. The young couple, pushing Julia in her stroller, were coming out and stopped to tell me that someone had left an X on the trail by crossing two large sticks, though their own hour-long search had not produced the quail dove.

Very strange. I hurried down the dusty path to the obvious signal—two crossed sticks arranged by some early-morning stranger. I carefully scrutinized the grassy borders, but discovered no dove feeding anywhere. Yet the silent message drew me back to the cross. I climbed down through brush and tangles into a trailside depression, a natural observation post where I could watch for movement in all directions.

A tall young man and his girlfriend strolled by and discovered my hunched-down figure, my arms hugging my knees, my body pressed against a vine-covered broken tree trunk. They peered inquiringly down through the crisscrossed vines that windowed my hideout.

"Have you heard about the quail dove?" I asked.

"Yes, we know that people have been searching for a strange bird."

"Will you help me look for it?"

"Yes," they assured me.

Holding hands, my newly enlisted scouts disappeared down Snake Bight Trail, but five minutes later the young man was back with this question: "Does it have a purplish-green head?"

"Yes, it does!" I shouted, and, scrambling up through the vines and roots, fell flat on my face at his feet. He laughed and bent down to help me pick myself up. We ran along the trail to where the girl pointed to a beautiful rust-brown bird, perfectly answering the description of the dove I was seeking, walking methodically through the brush, with feathers that looked so soft I wanted to stroke them.

"Thank you! Thank you!" Tears of joy splashed down my cheeks. I looked down and found myself standing on the palm frond I had placed in front of the fig tree!

My friends with the baby! Threatening to undo the stitches from recent knee surgery, I ran the half-mile back to the highway to tell them the good news. As we waved good-bye I suddenly realized that I had flown three thousand miles, driven eight hundred, and walked about twenty-five, and of all the people I had met I knew the name of only one—baby Julia.

SHARP EYES KEEP SHARP LOOKOUT FOR SHARP-TAIL

October 1979

The stars were still twinkling and white frost tinted the crisp leaves and grasses under my feet as the edge of night merged into pink streaks on the horizon. It was early October and my husband and I were the sole campers in Elk Island Provincial Park, close to the Canadian arctic in northern Alberta, where buffalo are still free to roam its thousands of acres. We had driven two thousand miles from Michigan because every year for the past three years a sharp-tailed sandpiper, a rare visitor from its Asian arctic breeding grounds, had been recorded around the tenth of October on the shores of Beaverhill Lake among the migrating pectoral sandpipers. We had asked many questions, checked details on our provincial maps, and plotted a course of action, and now we set out to find the sharp-tail.

Scouting the lakeshore six miles from the tiny village of Tofield turned out to be a hazardous business. Our station wagon had to cross a cut hay field (there was a cattle gate to open and close), navigate a narrow truck lane dangerously gutted into muddy ridges, and traverse an often disappearing track near the water's edge for several miles, where occasional stands of birch and poplar branches scritch-scratched noisily against our high-rise station wagon. Finally we arrived at a weir that separated the east and south shores and dammed up a small lake. Here is where our hopes lay. Here countless shorebirds, mostly dowitchers and pectoral sandpipers, stopped to feed on the muddy shore.

Our assumption that the job would be an easy one ended abruptly the first morning after we had hiked several miles of beach, carefully checking each shorebird for the marks of a fall-plumaged sharp-tailed sandpiper, which differs from the pectoral by its rusty cap, buffy breast, and lack of a sharply defined breast band. But it shares a preference for the higher-up shore areas instead of the shallow water where the dowitchers seldom lift their long, sturdy bills out of the water in their easily recognized rapid "sewing machine" feeding probes.

In and out of the grass clumps the pectoral sandpipers scurried. We scanned every inch of terrain and felt that we were identifying every bird, but a nagging doubt always remained. Flocks of pale winter-plumaged Lapland longspurs swooped down momentarily. Buffy, streak-breasted water pipits flitted, keeping us company all day long. A red-throated loon, a rarity in these parts, swam back and forth along the weir. The honking of Canada geese and a lone snow goose provided tundra background music. The dowitchers also kept up a clucking social conversation, and the pectorals complained, "Krik, krik" as they flushed and flew to other sections of the shore.

In late afternoon we gave up. That evening we telephoned Terry Thormin of the Provincial Museum of Alberta in Edmonton. He provided new information that guided us the following morning, after repeating the arduous journey to the lakeshore, to a chain of small islands parallel to the south shore of the lake. A tricky business indeed—our rubber boots squished down into a seemingly bottomless sea of soft muck. We had to wade across a narrow channel of swirling current between reed beds, with nothing to grab for support. But at last we reached "pec" colonies—dozens of individuals, some even feeding on open flats.

The day was sunny and calm, perfect for shorebirding. We attacked our project with vigor and enthusiasm, believing that now with such an abundant supply of candidates we would discover our bird in only a matter of minutes. In and out of the clumps of grass the little birds continued to hurry, as if racing the clock to fill up and be on their way south. Each scrutiny confirmed the dark bib of the "pec." The "dows" frequently sprang into the air, turned and twisted in unison, then settled down offshore again. Back to the mainland we sloshed, through the treacherous channel. A merlin startled us, darted into the reeds, then disappeared over the birch woods. We walked for miles and retraced our steps, but not a sharp-tail could we find.

One reward for the long day's vigil was the appearance of a pair of white-phase great horned owls, which we encountered in the poplar woods on our way back to camp. We jumped from our station wagon and followed them as they alternately perched and flew ahead of us, the pearl-gray of their pale feathers blending into the off-white of the poplar bark. This subspecies of the great horned owl is a specialty of the northwest.

The weather changed and brought a stiff northeast wind for the next day's birding, creating enormous curling whitecaps on the lake, bringing tears to our eyes and nearly disastrous footing in the channel. However, we crossed to the little islands and continued to search. After my ten-thousandth checkout I knew I would never doubt my identification of the size, shape, or field marks of a pectoral sandpiper!

This day our surprise visitor was a black gyrfalcon, which first swept low over the reeds, then zoomed directly toward us over the short prairie grass almost as if we were its target. The arrow-winged falcon shot away over the birch trees, and we did not see it again.

Weary from battling the wind, late in the afternoon we decided to extend our stay to the weekend, when Edmonton birders came out to see the red-throated loon, which still visited us daily near the weir. They would help us search for the sandpiper too.

Friday came. Rising in the dark, we drove the now familiar route and parked near the weir as dawn was breaking. We plodded through the mud to the islands, where under a peach-pink morning sky a large flock of "pecs" began their day of playing hide-and-seek with us. But we were tiring of their friendship. After a half hour of familiar greetings, suddenly a new acquaintance stepped out from behind a clump of grass and onto the mudflat, almost at our feet. A sharp-tail! The irregular soft streaks and buffy breast glowed in the light of the early sun. With unconcern it moved about under our gaze as if it were nothing special after all.

At that moment we felt an unexpected burst of cold wind and looked out over the lake of ominous choppy whitecaps, which were growing wilder by the minute. During our concentration on the busy sandpipers we had failed to notice how gray the sky had become. The water in the channel was rising fast, so we retreated, keeping our balance with difficulty on the perilous trip back to shore.

With the lowering clouds a curtain had descended, ending the play and turning the characters back into ordinary people who had to eat, sleep, and make decisions. We were terribly weary. We decided to start the long trek home.

Even as we drove away from the lake, a hawk owl flew toward us and perched on a farmer's wooden fence post! We had truly intertwined our lives with the dwellers of our earth on the edge of the arctic. Elk Island with its frosty dawn, the lake with its birch-lined shore, and the weir marking the end of the trail—all beckoned us to return.

ARIZONA HEAT WAVE

July 1980

Only extremely dedicated birders would abandon Michigan's famous Blue Water ideal vacation spots for Arizona's notorious summer blast-furnace climate in July, especially in a year that recorded the highest temperatures and longest heat wave ever. Yet, ignoring the headlines and alarming radio announcements, my husband and I stocked up on gallons of fruit juice and put extra ice cube trays in our travel-trailer freezer and, beginning each leg of our journey in the cool hours of the morning, covered the two-thousand-plus miles to Tucson in an easy three days. We were back in one of our favorite birding areas in North America: the Santa Rita, Huachuca, and Chiricahua mountain ranges.

The American Birding Association provides expert leadership to birders from all over the nation during three-day tours in limited habitats. The group brings a huge list of "wanted" birds, or more strongly expressed, "needed" birds. And therein lay the strong motivation for our invasion of the inhospitable world of our Southwest while our neighbors were refreshing themselves in the cool waters of Lake Huron.

Only in midsummer do a few rare hummingbirds cross the border from Mexico into North America during their post-breeding season. We "needed" them. Also at the top of our list was the zone-tailed hawk, which so far had defied our frequent attempts to locate one.

Our first target was the zone-tail. Our leader had heard about a nesting pair far up a canyon road. So one afternoon, in the hottest and quietest part of the day, he led the motorized caravan up a dusty road, where we left our vehicles to search for the nest. But almost immediately we spotted the two vulture-like hawks wheeling overhead, broad wings outstretched, black-and-white banded tails fanned out. As we traced their graceful soaring, they descended and alighted on treetops to inspect us and vocalize their objections to our visit. We soon withdrew.

Our second target was a violet-crowned hummingbird. This summer's only one had been reported at the famous Mile-High Nature Conservancy Lodge, where hummingbird feeders, filled daily, support a hummingbird population year round: black-chinned, blue-throated, rufous, Rivoli's, broad-billed, and Anna's. Our lone species among the regulars was the proverbial needle in a haystack. But Mile-Hi is an interesting place to be at any time, so we happily followed the narrow mountain road into Madera Canyon and settled down among the many feeders to watch the tiny colorful creatures flash red, blue, and green throats and hover with fantastically rapid wing-beats.

Zip! Zap! Zip! For an hour my eyes jumped restlessly from one flower-petaled tube to another until I could no longer fight off the descending-sun-drenched drowsiness. I had just pulled my big straw hat down over my eyes and relaxed against a low stone wall when a man's voice from far below us near a feeder hidden from our view called, "Violet-crown!" This was the payoff of the "many eyes" system. Our rare hummer wore a spotless white shirt and a brilliant violet cap, and his long bill glowed shining red.

You may wonder why we involved ourselves with such oppressive weather conditions in order to see just two new birds. Actually, we tried for a third, a very unlikely target—a buff-collared nightjar, a brownish version of our whip-poor-will but that sounds entirely different. Only one or two pairs have ever been found north of the Mexican border and by July are absolutely silent and almost impossible to locate. However, one night we observers, carpooling in six vehicles, started up Guadalupe Canyon near the New Mexico border. Our graveled county highway became a narrow dirt canyon road. We rocked and rolled down into stony, dry washes, ever deeper into the canyon. Not the moon nor a star shone in the sky. Scudding clouds glowered; lightning streaked from sky to earth. The trail ended, and silently, our dark figures emerged from the cars onto the edge of the road.

Our leader, in familiar home territory, confidently stepped into the canyon. Stumbling after him, we followed. For two hours we proceeded cautiously in the dark as we listened for the call of a nightjar. Our attempt was a long shot that failed. But a western screech owl came in to observe us. In the glare of our lantern he tipped on the branch until he stared at us with head hanging down in a most ludicrous pose, lightening the moment by making us laugh.

Laughter turned into near panic on the return trip. Steady raindrops had penetrated our canyon; within minutes the dry washes became flooded. The road surface could be described only as "greasy"—worse than sheet ice. At a crawling pace and endlessly skidding from one far side to the other, our heroic drivers did not lose control of a single vehicle. After what seemed like ages, the wide county road regained, our dauntless band, long after midnight, faced another predawn field trip!

I have always been intrigued by parrots, parakeets, motmots, and trogons, which to me suggest mysterious rivers, tangled jungles, and the forest traffic of stealthy animals. Several years before, we had camped in the South Fork of Cave Creek Canyon and had seen and photographed an elegant trogon. Now, near our campground at Boggs Spring in Madera Canyon, where my husband was occupied trying to identify the dozen or so hummingbirds clustered around our syrup feeder, I was unprepared for a faint "quark" that instantly evoked a distant memory.

I waited. A few minutes later I heard another "quark." It was enough to start me on a quest that led to a narrow dry canyon and alternate periods of listening and waiting as I quietly moved closer to the source of the low "quark, quark, quark" somewhere in a tree along the canyon edge. Bridled titmice, western wood pewees, and olivaceous flycatchers furnished background music, almost obnoxiously since my concentration was aimed at a colorful, tropical rarity. Then, from an exposed branch of a tall tree on the opposite side of the canyon, an elegant trogon, with his glistening green body, bright rose belly, and long, square-cut tail with a black band across the tip, looked down at me. A collar of white edged the green throat, and altogether he was a handsome and imposing sight. It was awfully exciting to track down my very own elegant trogon.

We extended our trip for another day when we heard of a known spotted owl nesting area in Garden Canyon. With several friends we decided to make a daytime climb up the mountain, wearing rugged boots and carrying plenty of water. The steady ascent, initially steep, wound through sycamore and other deciduous trees, followed a trail along a dry streambed, occasionally necessitated taking a flying leap from one rock to another, or gripping a helping hand from above or extending one to a fellow traveler below. Hot air drifted from the rocks. We seemed to encounter no pine habitat, preferred by spotted owls, but everybody scrutinized the limbs of every large tree for the familiar owl shape. At last the canyon merged with a trail, and we began to see dark ponderosa pines ahead.

Dr. Paul MacKenzie, of Kingston, Ontario, moved away from the group and continued up the dry streambed. If he had not done so, I would have missed one of the most fantastic bird sightings of my lifetime. Skirting the right edge of the ravine, Paul almost ran into the pair.

This time nobody shouted. Only six hardy climbers had made it to the top. While we waited for the stragglers to appear, we tiptoed to a gray rock ledge and rested, leaning against tree trunks. The spotted owls blinked but did not move. They were royalty of the bird world: fearless, mighty, beautiful. The vivid memory of them is a picture engraved in my mind.

An enlarged photograph of two enormous brown owls—pressed close together, dark eyes open wide—framed and displayed on a wall in our home is our reward for conquering Arizona in the summertime.

BIRD #700

July 1980

Oh yes, the beavers. I thought I knew all about beavers. Beavers gnaw at poplar trees until they topple, then push and pile them across streams until the water behind the scraggly barriers can no longer run downstream. Thus a beaver pond is born.

I remember well watching the fading glow of sunset from a leaf-strewn knoll at Beaver Dam Campground in the Canadian Rockies on our way home from a camping trip late one August; the beavers still paddled tirelessly back and forth, back and forth. Each glistening, bewhiskered brown swimmer carried a stick between his front teeth, adding it to the already well-mounded winter condominium. An earsplitting blast shattered the evening's peace and quiet, and we jerked forward in time to see the crisp slap of a beaver tail on the water. Then a second time bomb ripped the still evening. I have been told this is a warning signal in beaverland.

Then there was Ausable Lake, high in the Adirondack mountain meadow, where we portaged our canoes around small pilings until we emerged on top of the world onto a mile-long trout-filled empoundment that had been created by beavers. We fished for "brookies" from under the brushy coves and thanked the lake engineers.

Even in Ontario, along the Bruce Trail where we used to backpack on Memorial Day weekends, the pointed, freshly toothed stumps on the edge of the marsh proclaimed a beaver civilization, while we, with hand magnifiers, crawled on hands and knees and found the tiny twayblade blossoms.

But Colorado's beaver construction truly amazed us as we drove south from the city of Evergreen. Tier after tier, mile upon mile, the dams and their backed-up quiet pools decorated both edges of pine-forested roads. For how many eons had the Sammy Beavers gnawed, toted, paddled, and stacked—and slapped their strong, broad tails?

And the tall, dark, thick pine forests reminded me of campgrounds in northern California, Oregon, Minnesota, and our own Michigan's Upper Peninsula. But wait a minute; this is supposed to be a bird story!

By now you may have guessed that I was desperately trying to push bird #700 out of my mind. Our target, the flammulated owl, had eluded us on so many occasions; for example, taunting us from dense pine trees in the Santa Rita Mountains of Arizona, or refusing to answer a taped call in the Chiricahuas. Since we already knew this "flamm" had a nest somewhere in the birch opening deep on an old logging trail, I somehow felt I was on my way to an appointment. But this meeting was special.

We finally stopped driving and began walking around in a poplar grove. Spear-shaped pines still darkened the forest ceiling; shafts of sunlight flicked shadows on our faces. If we noticed a nesting hole in a tree, we had merely to tap gently on the tree trunk and hope the little dark-eyed owl would pop out to investigate us.

But that devious trick proved unnecessary. We had walked for only a few minutes when my husband quietly called to me, "Here he is—perched outside his hole!" The little bird had kept his appointment with us! The flammulated owl stared at us, downy brown and white with slightly ruffled breast feathers, all five and a half inches of him serenely indifferent to our gaze. He obviously did not feel threatened, so we stared back, imprinting into our memories the rusty discs surrounding the dark eyes and the camouflage of gray and black birch bark.

As I trained my binoculars on the diminutive bird from a discreet distance, I wondered what I would remember most about this encounter. One tends to think of owls as large, secretive, nocturnal predators. I was impressed by this tiny fellow's niche deep in the great forest. This owl prefers forests of ponderosa pine. It feeds on moths, beetles, and spiders taken at the end of swift flights to branches and foliage, then perches inconspicuously next to the tree trunk.

We dragged ourselves away. He had been a very difficult target throughout the years, and we hated to let him go. But as his soft feathery outline melted into the background of his round doorway, I felt certain that if I returned someday, Mr. Flamm would still be living here and wouldn't at all mind if I dropped in to say hello.

Once upon a time I had hoped for a very rare seven-hundredth bird for my life list. Possibly a bristle-thighed curlew, a spoon-billed sandpiper, or a Mongolian plover. But birding is only a game, to be played forever as partners continue to roam meadows, hike trails, climb mountains, wade rivers, or relax by quiet streams, and everywhere follow the flash of tantalizing feathers.

We couldn't have had a more wonderful day!

INVASION OF THE GREAT GRAY OWLS

January 1982

Some rare birds seem to elude one an entire lifetime, and sometimes one is privileged a second glimpse of a very special species. Seldom does the great gray owl come as far south as Michigan, but the weekend of January 28, 1982, we learned that not only one, but several great grays had been found on Neebish Island, fifteen miles south of Sault Ste. Marie in Michigan's Upper Peninsula. My husband was confined to bed with a terrible cold and was unable to travel, but a phone call to my friends the indomitable Defevers, Charlie and Florence, was enough to set a plan in motion. We were on our way before dawn, our lunches packed and thermoses filled with coffee and tea, with down jackets, wool caps and scarves, heavy boots, and warm gloves piled on the backseat, all set for the seven-hour drive to the "Soo."

Fortunately, the day was calm, the roads clear. Still, it was a long piece till the silver-gray supports and cables of the "Mighty Mac" Mackinac Bridge etched themselves against the sky. Suspense built up as we crossed the bridge, cut east, continued north on the highway, and at last headed east again on a smaller road. Our informant had directed us to the ferry dock, where to our dismay we viewed only open water!

But some kind soul had jammed a wooden stick into the shore ice, and on it hung a white cardboard sign that read FOLLOW THE ROW OF CHRISTMAS TREES. Through our binoculars we spotted eight or ten small evergreen trees spaced at intervals across a snowy stretch of frozen river half a mile upstream.

Back to the road we hurried; it was nearly two o'clock in the afternoon. Charlie opted to guard the car (later he found a log cabin bar on the far side of the highway) while Florence and I prepared to cross the half-mile of river and hike as far as necessary on Neebish Island on the other side. Florence pulled a red snowmobile suit over her layers of woolens. I added a mountain parka over my down jacket. We both tied scarves around our necks and faces as we began to slide over the ice, which was a trifle scary as we eyed the open water to the right. But snowmobile tracks stretching out ahead reassured us that our footing ought to be safe.

With a sense of relief we climbed up the slippery bank of the island and started up a road guarded by dense woods on either side. Our first encounter was with a road maintenance snowplow driver. He informed us that the owls could be seen about a mile farther up the road, near an old house where they often perched on fence posts. Cheered by this good news, we trudged on. Our second encounter was with a woman, an island resident who stopped her car to chat with us. She told us that she drove the route daily to pick up mail and often saw the owls—but not *every* day. For the first time we realized with dismay that we might not find the big owls.

I elected to check out a snowfield and also watch for a black-backed three-toed woodpecker or a boreal chickadee. Florence chose to catch a ride. Shortly after the car disappeared over a hill, I spotted my great gray owl, which was leaning forward attentively like a broken tree stump in the white meadow. A few seconds later the owl spread his huge wings and flew to a perch on top of a weathered wooden fence post. And there he remained, turning his enormous head, blinking his yellow eyes, and showing off his white bow tie.

Now I was concerned that Florence would miss the bird, so I hurried on until I could see her, a tiny red spot in the distance. I wanted to share my fabulous sighting with her. She wasn't moving. In fact, while I covered the mile as quickly as I could, occasionally waving my arms to get her attention, she seemed glued to the spot. Finally I was close enough to shout, "Have you found an owl?" She still did not turn, but pointed to a small tree directly in front of her. There sat her own great gray owl, so close she could almost have touched his feathers. She had seen it first from the car. But to her disappointment, a shrike flew at it and the owl flew into the woods. Then, unexpectedly, it flew back again, directly toward her, almost touching her, and landed in the tree alongside the road. I believe she memorized every line of his facial discs, white throat feathers, and brown barrings while she guarded her prize for me.

Darkness comes early in January in the Northern Hemisphere. Jubilantly, we started our return journey, but now we faced into the wind. Then the onslaught of a blinding snowstorm began suddenly, with a freezing wind that battered at our eyes, and soon white flakes lodged in our lashes, the only exposed area of our bodies. Those beautiful lacy stars that delight us when they decorate the early-morning frosted windows of winter now blinded us. We bent into the glittering whiteness, the gradual descending road our only guide to the river.

As the late afternoon drop in temperature nipped at us, little did we know rescue was at hand, sent by Charlie from the safety of the warm bar—a teenage boy on a red snowmobile drove up and offered to ferry us back to the mainland. Florence was brave enough to go first, climbing up behind the driver, and was whisked out of sight in seconds. Before I had time to round the last bend, the boy was back, and I clung to him desperately as we flew, bounced, jounced, and covered the distance in ten minutes that would have taken us an hour or more to traverse on foot.

But Florence and I agreed that battling the elements had enhanced the satisfaction of finding our very own great gray owl. So off to the bar and a toast to our success!

PART III
ALASKA

HOME AT GLACIER BAY

July 1973

Glacier Bay National Monument is unique in our national park system. For three hundred years naturalists have recorded the recession of the glaciers with the accompanying exposure of bays and inlets; studied the history of past ages; and witnessed the stages of plant life beginning anew from the first lichens, moss, and dryas to the climax forests of hemlock and spruce.

Glacier Bay can be reached by plane from Juneau, Alaska, and one day in early July, my husband, our son Matt, his friend Jeff, and I climbed aboard after checking our backpacks, which contained lightweight tents and food enough for four days of wilderness camping. This was our first stop on a summerlong camping trip. Propellers whirred, we climbed laboriously into the air, and then below there was nothing but water and rocky islands. We were going backward in time to the bare surface of the earth as it was before life as we know it existed, to the beginnings of geological history.

As we approached Glacier Bay Lodge by shuttle bus from the

airstrip, the driver stopped at the edge of the bay and pointed down the shore. "Bartlett Cove is about a quarter mile," he announced helpfully while we shouldered our backpacks, already staring in wonderment at the beauty of the bay, the moss-laden spruce forest and snow-covered mountain range, and focusing binoculars on a pigeon guillemot riding the waves offshore.

Matt, Jeff, and I reached the camping area first. There were no regular spaces; campers had to search for a flat, smooth spot in the woods for a tent site and claim a rock-encircled fire bowl on the beach. To keep out of the reach of bears, food was safely stored in a hinged box and hoisted high into a tree. The boys had already pitched their tents when my husband finally arrived. A blue grouse with her chicks had wandered onto his path, and he had been lying on his stomach photographing them. A giant flat rock on the beach made a wonderful picnic table, where we loafed in the sunshine, admiring our new home. Surprise! A few hours later our piece of natural furniture had disappeared under the high tide!

We were free to explore our domain, where a varied thrush trilled from the forest, a chestnut-backed chickadee chipped among the leaves, and seabirds journeyed back and forth in the sky over the bay. We hiked the beach path through wild gardens of Indian paintbrush, hid behind the lofty dark tree trunks to watch baby goldeneyes swimming on Black Pond, and hopefully searched the spruce heights for a three-toed woodpecker. Only a few other campers appeared at Bartlett Cove—three young ladies stopped by to inform us that bears are fond of plastic bread wrappers (personal experience), and a young man taking his bride camping for the first time rushed over to borrow some salt.

But the object of our presence here was to see the glaciers up close, and for that we reserved space on Captain Watson's sightseeing boat, the *Seacrest*. We planned to ask the captain to put us ashore to camp near the glaciers and pick us up the following day; though we had thought about this for a long time, it was a difficult decision to make, as several years earlier the park rangers had moved their summer quarters to tents erected on floating barges offshore after some annoying experiences with grizzly bears. Yet we had dreamed of exploring in the footsteps of John Muir, so we repacked our backpacks for an overnight stay and set our alarm clock for an early awakening to be certain we'd reach the dock on time.

The *Seacrest* departed promptly at eight o'clock, carrying some thirty passengers. Captain Watson soon displayed his expertise on everything about Glacier Bay: its history, its geography, and its animal and bird life. He pointed to bird cliffs, an eagle's nest, newborn seals sunning themselves on ice floes, and mountain goats grazing on high meadows. Flocks of tiny northern phalaropes settled like clouds of mosquitoes on the water, while marbled and Kittlitz's murrelets skittered out of our way.

For five hours the little ship steamed along. Maud Tyson, generous hostess, served soup and sandwiches, offering the boys all the seconds and thirds they could consume and completely winning their affection. At last Riggs Glacier emerged in the distance, and as we approached, no words can describe the sequence of expectancy, power, grandeur, loneliness, and admiration that claimed our emotions. The newly exposed glacial surfaces glistened blue, their crystals so compressed they could not absorb light. Great weight pressed the ice into folds and fissures. We sailed among icebergs sculptured into towers, ships, ice-cream cones, whales, and hundreds of other, indescribable images. A magnificent explosion reverberated as if it were caged within canyon walls when a piece of the glacier separated and slid irrevocably into the tidewater.

Soon after we chugged away from Riggs Glacier, Captain Watson lowered his skiff near Goose Cove, and the first mate rowed us ashore, first Matt and Jeff with their packs, then my husband and me. We were abandoned on the sandy beach as astonished eyes stared at us over the rails of the receding cruise boat and a few passengers waved farewell.

The habitat was a sandy, alder-covered beach tucked behind a jutting precipice and rimmed by a mountain chain. Creeks emptied into the cove, creating gravel deltas. And we made certain to pitch our light nylon tents safely above the high-tide line. The boys had permission to explore wherever they wished while my husband and I quickly climbed from rock to rock, ascending a streambed that led to an alpine meadow, on our way to tundra ponds where we hoped to find nesting red-throated loons.

We circled several small lakes. Sanderlings flew up, trying to distract us by crying piteously and pretending to have broken wings. Our path angled along a ridge into a neighboring valley, up and over the summit of a second crest, and through meadow grass and rocky outcrops until it emerged above a vast expanse of bogs and ponds below. And on one of the ponds swam a pair of red-throated loons, sweetly graceful in their wild isolation.

I rested against a grassy hummock on the mountain. My husband descended to the lake and, shielded by alder thickets, slowly approached until he caught the proud beauty of the loons in his camera lens. He rejoined me, and we began our return journey to camp.

Clouds had replaced sunshine, and a light rain misted down. We retraced our steps through the pass. We crossed over the saddle and sighted a streambed in the distance, but on nearing it we found alders so dense that the valley was impenetrable.

Confidently, we worked our way up the next saddle, but instead of returning to our cove we found ourselves again looking down on the loon lake!

We had oriented ourselves by the reddish mountain southeast of our campsite, so we tried to keep it behind us; but our every effort to discover the trail back to Goose Cove met with frustration. We rested and deliberated on our predicament, and decided to continue in a straight line until we reached the bay, follow the shore in the direction of the headland, and climb to the top. The high ridge would lead us back to an area where we could spot our tents from above.

The rain steadily increased as we found the beach and traversed the sandy shoreline until we reached the headland, where curls of white foam crashed and returned surging to the sea, preventing further travel. Clutching the wet but sturdy alder roots, we somehow pulled ourselves to the summit. There the ground leveled off, and the rest of the course led us along the cliff edge. We were forced to continually bear left so we wouldn't take a catastrophic fall into the ocean. Breaking through the twisted alder thicket was like prying our way through a tangled jungle. Our fingers grew numb from clawing at the thick, cold branches. Progress was slow, and it was disheartening to check the shore below and realize how far inland we had to go to work our way to safety.

Our heads, jeans, and boots were thoroughly soaked. By eleven o'clock we had been walking for eight hours, most of the time over mountainous terrain. Alaska's arctic night light was a blessing.

Just as we despaired of reaching camp before morning, we heard the boys' voices! Our answer rang out, and a man's voice urged, "Stay on the ridge!"

Matt and Jeff had reported to the ranger on his raft out in

the bay our failure to return. A wonderful warm sensation of relief flooded us; we knew that we were no longer alone and lost. Half an hour later, Clarence Summers, a national park ranger, arrived with the boys to lead us down the face of the steep mountain, slipping and sliding on the loose talus slope, and finally cutting through the last band of alders to familiar ground.

"Motherrr! We were worried about you!" Isn't it supposed to be the other way around with teenagers?

We were exhausted, but we needed food and warmth. Mike Nigra, the other ranger, rowed in to shore to pick us up. I was so surprised to be met at the raft by his pretty wife, Debbie, that I forgot my weariness. Debbie cut slices of still-warm banana bread she had baked for us, to eat with scrambled eggs and hot chocolate. Was I dreaming, standing here, not cold and wet on the mountain any longer?

Later Mike rowed us ashore. My hips had rusty hinges instead of joints, but doggedly I placed one foot in front of the other, not even looking ahead until the bright orange tent signaled our campsite. My down sleeping bag was warm and dry. I don't remember anything else, for I was already fast asleep.

The next morning I opened my eyes and wondered where I was. Eleven o'clock! Sunshine! I could walk! We built a fire and breakfasted on hot oatmeal with brown sugar. Our wilderness home seemed lovely and secure. Shy golden-crowned sparrows serenaded us from the sheltering alders. We explored the Goose Cove delta and found nesting semipalmated plovers and gray-crowned rosy finches.

Too soon the *Seacrest* stood offshore, and the skiff ferried us and our belongings away from the never-to-be-forgotten Goose Cove. Passengers hung over the rail, watching curiously while we clumsily swung ourselves over the stern. The boys headed for the galley and their friend Maud, who didn't disappoint them. We were back at Bartlett Cove in time for dinner.

We knew our home at Glacier Bay would remain an unforgettable memory, but we promised ourselves *never* again to go exploring without a topographical map!

HOME ON ST. LAWRENCE ISLAND

July 1973

I couldn't believe that we were looking down on the coast of Siberia as our tiny plane flew low over the Bering Sea to St. Lawrence Island, home of a few hundred Inuit living in two small villages. Wrapped in layers of arctic outerwear, we had been delayed most of the day, waiting in the Nome airport for the weather to clear. At four o'clock in the afternoon, our pilot, wearing jeans and a light corduroy jacket, had thrown our backpacks on top of a sack of mail and some cartons of soft drinks destined for the government store, and we had climbed aboard. Now he was looking for a hole in the clouds so that we could land.

I wasn't frightened, because I knew that arctic flights are played by ear; that is, the bush pilot makes all the decisions about whether to fly or land. Just when I was sure that we would be forced to return to Nome, we dropped into a bank of gray fog and down onto a narrow, sandy landing strip bounded by the ocean on one side and a mile-long lake on the other. We were in the village of Gambell.

At the sound of the plane overhead a dozen villagers, dressed in fur-trimmed parkas and traveling on all-terrain vehicles, had gathered to view the unloading. We held no confirmation of a reservation and had had no answer to our letter requesting accommodations on the island. So we hesitantly asked a bystander to point out the home of Vernon Slwooko, who we had heard from the Alaska Airlines agent in Nome had rooms to rent. The bystander pointed to the far end of the village.

The village was a fair distance away, and at every step our boots sank into the stony surface of the ground. Bending into the wind, we laboriously progressed past freshly dug holes in the earth, a far-flung scattering of bleached whale bones, and unpainted houses, a church, a store, racks of drying fish, and the village well. Finally we reached a group of six small houses built by the Federal Aviation Administration during World War II and now sadly in a state of disrepair. They had been purchased by Vernon Slwooko with money he had earned as a guide for Jacques Cousteau.

Stocky, crew-cut Vernon Slwooko zoomed up on his ATV and introduced us to our new home, one of the unpainted houses opposite his own small house. Originally, we had thought of tenting on the island; now we realized how lucky we were to have a small bedroom with its two iron cots, an oil heater in the tiny living room, a wooden table with four wooden chairs, a single lightbulb hanging from the ceiling, and an adequate water supply stored in pails.

From our ice-packed front steps, the nearby village and its surroundings appeared to be a painting: gray, unmoving, and unchanging. The arctic evening sky was still light. We bundled up in heavy jackets and wool caps, although it was July, and threaded our way among the unfamiliar shanties to the shore, using as our landmarks the walrus-skin boats stored upside down on the high wooden racks near the beach.

By now it was eleven o'clock at night and dusky as we looked out over the Bering Sea. A dark shape flew in front of us over the water. We lifted our binoculars. There were many dark shapes, then dozens, then hundreds, yes, millions of birds flying in a continuous stream on their nightly feeding flight from their nests on the mountain cliffs. There were more birds than I had ever dreamed inhabited the whole world!

The next morning we climbed to the top of the mountain. There, seabirds circled our heads, whirring, landing, chattering, and scolding. Crested, parakeet, and least auklets; puffins; and murre parents deserted their stone watchtowers when we neared, but the youngsters posed unblinking and unafraid.

Black rocks bordered the lakeshore, but we could follow a footpath that sometimes entered the watery inlets. Everywhere snow bunting and Lapland longspurs carried food to their young. Baird's and rock sandpipers pecked purposefully along the water's edge.

Every day we examined the many deep middens, the cave-like holes where local inhabitants dug for ancient ivory carvings and Stone Age tools, and where birds could be found resting from the long migration flight. The round pebbles underfoot slipped and slid continually until our legs ached so much that we had to stop to rest.

Vernon and his wife, Beda, became our friends. Beda and I bartered. The government store was completely out of everything, its shelves empty from floor to ceiling, but the villagers daily expected the arrival of the government boat, the *North Star,* with a years' replenishment of supplies. I had brought food enough to last for our expected four-day stay, but I needed sandwich material, so I exchanged a can of potato salad for a loaf of bread. Beda offered to make sealskin slippers for me in exchange for enough corduroy to make a parka, to be ordered from Penney's catalog. She scraped a sealskin for us and decorated it with beads and quills, and we promised to send copies of pictures we had taken.

Villagers came to call. Franklin, the mayor, and his wife, Martha, came one evening. He told us of his hopes for the growth of the village and described the first prefabricated house expected on the next barge. Eight-year-old Gilbert and his mother came to sell us small prehistoric artifacts that they had found during their summer digging. I bought a small seabird, shaped by the skillful hands of a Stone Age man, its brown color confirming its age. The women and children of St. Lawrence Island spend much of their time digging up the fossil ivory from sites where earlier civilizations lived in the warmth of underground dwellings. These items are valued by museum directors and are a source of income for the island people. The ivory carvers of St. Lawrence Island are famous, and from the storekeeper we purchased a beautifully carved snowy owl mounted on a piece of fossilized bone.

When Vernon agreed to take us in his walrus-skin boat thirty-five miles down the coast to explore a large lagoon, day after day we had to keep reminding him because he was so busy. He had to make the weather reports to the mainland, as his wireless set was the island's only contact with the outside world. He had to meet the mail plane, fill the family water jugs, and take time for many cups of tea. But one noon when he had finished his errands, he rushed down to the beach on his ATV and deposited the motor, oars, fishing pole, and rifle in his boat. An hour later Vernon; his nineteen-year-old son, Archie; his fourteen-year-old daughter, Roberta; my husband; and some helpful neighbors joined to push the heavy boat over the beach stones on two wooden rollers and into the surf. We were on our way in an ancient craft, built from walrus skins and whalebone, that appeared unwieldy but rode the waves so well that we traveled comfortably all afternoon.

We sailed past old fishing camps and a rock-strewn shore, where Vernon, with the experienced touch of a lifetime seafarer, nudged the boat in so close to the rafts of seabirds that my husband could photograph at close range thick-billed murres, red phalarope, and common eiders. In the late afternoon we reached the lagoon and had time to walk, fish, and eat. On our hike inland we sighted a male king eider silently rocking on a tundra pond.

We returned to the beach and rested. My arms hugged my knees, and I gazed out over the sea at the constant motion of birds, waves, and sometimes a gray whale surfacing close to shore, while Vernon described the fishing camps his ancestors used to make. He told us about the ducks and geese that nest on the inaccessible interior of his island, and he described the process of building a walrus-skin boat. On the long nighttime ride back to the village, loons, gulls, and jaegers flew overhead.

But our four days were up, and the day came to fly out. Mist touched the ground that morning, and our mountain was entirely hidden. We carried our belongings to the small wooden shed that served as an airport, hoping for a change in the weather so Munz Airline's pilot Otis would be able to land, but it never came. Vernon came to tell us the bad news. Unfortunately, we had consumed the last of our carefully rationed food supply. We decided to camp out in the airport shack until the plane could come in.

The morning brought good news. The *North Star*, the once-a-year supply ship, was due at noon. We read the announcement on a sheet of yellow paper that had been fastened onto the door of the general store. Already children were streaming to the beach. We could see the ship far out at anchor and sensed the excitement as families hurried to view the unloading. The men had all signed up to lift incoming freight from the ship's barges and pile it on wooden sleds that were pulled by the town's one tractor. This was an uncommon and welcome opportunity for them to earn money.

The sleds scraped endlessly back and forth over the sand. Supplies for the store came first, and the store remained open until midnight so the villagers could purchase the canned goods they had been so long without. And we bought baked beans and canned hot dogs for our dinner. When night arrived, we stretched our sleeping bags out on the wooden floor of the little shed, where we were protected from the crosswinds that whipped over the landing strip.

Again the heavy mist did not lift. For a second day the sleds ceaselessly ferried boxes and bundles of all shapes and sizes: ATVs, Hondas, swing sets, motor parts, furniture, lumber, and long-awaited packages from mail-order houses. The men of the island had pieced together a long pipeline in order to pump a year's supply of gasoline into storage tanks. And we were glad that we could buy another canned dinner, though at an extraordinarily high price.

A third day of waiting arrived. The mountain was clear. Hurray! However, waves from the sea crashed menacing spray as we slogged toward the village to get the weather report from Vernon. "Maybe today," he offered. "Maybe not. Too much wind." So we spent another day reading and walking for hours, blown about by the great wind. Even Otis, a fearless pilot, dared not try to bring his plane down in this weather. Stephen and Susan Braund, University of Alaska students who were writing a thesis on the subject of skin boats, invited us to dinner in their Quonset hut. It was a real party of corned beef hash and deep-fried fritters cooked on a camp stove. Dessert was our donation of a can of peaches.

A new day dawned on our confining shelter. We had instant coffee and biscuits with jelly for breakfast. Vernon's prediction was: "Otis comes today, maybe." And late in the day Otis came, gliding down on a twenty-five-knot wind, under a four-hundred-foot ceiling, his flying giant insect lurching along the windy runway and slamming to a halt at the door of our castle.

We waved good-bye to Vernon, Stephen, Susan in her fur-lined parka, and all the other smiling faces, the Inuit of St. Lawrence Island, who had walked with us on the beaches, visited us in our temporary home, invited us to their camps, and shared with us their heritage. They are our brothers and sisters.

FIRST EXPLORATORY TRIP TO ATTU ISLAND

May 1977

The Reeves Aleutian Super Electra winged away over the snowcapped mountains, leaving our party of eleven birders on the runway on Attu Island, last of the Aleutian Islands chain, two thousand miles from mainland Alaska. Near the runway loomed the Coast Guard station, off limits to us, and the loran tower, which is manned twenty-four hours a day, sending long-range navigational signals to airplanes and ships at sea. On the nearby landscape mangled, twisted ruins of storage tanks, dismembered vehicles, and rusted runway mesh lay scattered everywhere, a reminder of the grim days of World War II, when American troops fought the Japanese invaders in bitter battles. Sea-washed timbers from devastated buildings bordered the shore. Along old winding roads, half buried in the hillsides, jutted dozens of rust-brown, doorless Quonset huts. Around us, the melting spring snow created little ponds on the tundra where dwarf willows sprouted downy gray buds.

High on a hill opposite the loran tower stood one magnificent ruin, a shattered, battered, partly roofless remnant of a gymnasium, windowless and ghostly gray with age. Cold air seeped through its splintered siding, and near the front entrance one could make out the now almost obliterated yellow letters: ATTU SPORTS PALACE. This was to be our home for the next ten days, ten keen birdmen and I.

A Coast Guard truck arrived with our luggage. I looked over the pile, then carefully searched again. My backpack was not there! In dismay I shivered in the cold mist, unable to comprehend this predicament! The airplane would not return for another week. I peered down at my arctic traveling clothes. I had departed from Michigan on a warm May day, wearing thermal underwear, wool slacks, a wool shirt, wool socks, insulated boots, a mountain parka, a wool cap, and wool-lined leather gloves, and I carried a down-filled jacket. In the pocket of my jacket, I found a small flashlight, a whistle, a jackknife, a notebook and pencil, a bandana, and a lipstick. In my small canvas day pack, which I had worn on the plane, I found a pair of hip boots, a rainsuit, a pint thermos, and a can of talcum powder.

The executive officer of the Coast Guard station patted me on my shoulder as he explained that he'd just learned that my backpack had been accidentally unloaded at Shemya Air Force Base, which had been our only stop along the way. He hurried away and returned with an olive-drab down sleeping bag, a red sweatshirt and a pair of men's thermal underwear for me to sleep in, a toothbrush, and two pairs of his own wool socks. For a whole week?

We bridged precarious gaping holes in the floor of the old gymnasium with wooden slats. We pitched two-man Timberline tents in the dry sections. With a trestle table and wooden benches we fashioned a bleak dining room, and on one end of the table we established our kitchen, four single-burner gas units. An adjacent table and bench stored our rations: packets of instant oatmeal, cartons of pilot biscuits, peanut butter and jelly, Pop-Tarts, dehydrated dinners, eggs, pancake mix, granola bars, coffee, tea, and instant hot chocolate.

As we established our indoor campsite, among the disreputable debris in a corner I discovered a stained and dusty mattress, which I carefully wrapped with a piece of plastic and dragged into our tent. At least I had a wonderful bed.

As soon as the tents had been pitched, though the rain still misted down we eagerly began our first exploratory walk into a valley where a rare, migratory Asian bird had been discovered the day before. We left the shore and half-circled a large lake. We descended into a marshy area of the Henderson River, named Massacre Valley from its war history, where we were walled in by snow-covered mountains. We continued our search among a stand of leafless willows, and here, at last, we all got a good view of the chunky, pink-breasted little finch as it fluttered in and about the bushes. We named the area Bullfinch Valley in honor of our first new bird, and so the name remains to this day.

On our return, we followed a path that led to the shore and hiked back along a dirt road that had once been maintained as part of a U.S. Army base. Remnants of wooden docks, dynamited by the departing soldiers, provided perching places for seabirds, colonies of red-faced and pelagic cormorants. By the time we reached the Sports Palace, we had walked many miles on our day of arrival.

But the next morning we packed lunches and began another hike, to Alexei Point. The trek began at the end of the long airplane runway, continued along the indented mountainous coast, and ended several miles later at the end of a rock-strewn road on a marshy triangle of land. On the return journey, participants, many unused to hiking, trudged slowly with sore, blistered feet, only to hear that a hawfinch had been sighted up the hill near a deserted, dilapidated concrete building. Though everybody dashed off and searched the surrounding meadows, the hawfinch was not seen again. Thoroughly miserable, we returned to our cold, dreary shelter. But the incident lived on and became the famous Hawfinch Death March. (Years later, on a pelagic outing off North Carolina, I encountered a participant who was wearing a T-shirt with a logo printed on the back: I SURVIVED THE HAWFINCH DEATH MARCH.)

At first the crisscrossed old roads were confusing. Later the ditches that were filled with rusted metal, demolished vehicles, wire, and useless motors; the crushed storage tanks; a few remaining weathered wooden uprights; and a field of broken runway mesh all became useful landmarks. The Henderson and Peaceful river valleys penetrated into the mountain ranges where white-tailed sea eagles sometimes soared. A four-mile route along the shore in the other direction passed Casco Cove, a landing strip for shorebirds, on its way to Murder Point, where with a telescope a lucky sea-watcher might spy even an albatross over the white-capped ocean.

A freezing rain descended on the third and fourth days but did not deter scouting expeditions around the island. In fact, rain became a daily factor, reappearing so suddenly at the most unexpected moments that we never started anywhere without carrying rain gear. Wearing rubber boots allowed us to wade ponds and streams overflowing now with melting ice. The land was utterly brown. Snow edged the path between the Sports Palace and the sea. The gymnasium retained the night's coldness, and if we did return to it at lunchtime, we preferred to dine on our soup, crackers, and cheese while sitting on the outside steps in the weak sunshine.

The distances between areas to be searched were so great

that three walkie-talkies were in use. One remained at the Palace and the other two were carried by separate birding parties. Each hour we made contact. Some days no new sightings were reported. But sometimes a rare species turned up in the marsh or dwarf willows, or among the ruins of Navy Town. Then everybody converged on the area before the target disappeared. Those were exciting times.

One morning the weather was just too raw for a birding foray. But after lunch two hours of reading was enough for me. I donned rain gear and began a slow walk over the meadow, where a mile of rusted mesh grating indicated the presence of a former aircraft landing strip. I brushed through overgrown patches of weeds, kicked at the broken wires, and suddenly saw what looked like a robin, hiding in the circle of a roll of rusty fencing. But it couldn't be a robin. A thrush? Davis Finch had also decided to roam about in the rain, and I ran to him, calling about my find. Together, we found the bird again, and it was an eyebrowed thrush! Carefully, we spread out to guard but not frighten the little gray-feathered, pink-breasted bird. The word was out, and one by one everybody came until they all had seen the unexpected rare find.

Our small group became good friends. We shared the constant search for new birds and we shared the housekeeping chores. In the evenings we inscribed our field notes or discussed the field marks of the species we had seen or those we hoped to see. My only memory of real warmth was almost immediately after crawling into my sleeping bag. After our long days' labors, I hardly waited to feel its comfort before I was sound asleep.

There is always great speculation about the plane arrival on Attu; sometimes because of stormy weather the plane cannot land for weeks. The day before our departure we experienced a lashing downpour and extremely low visibility. But the next morning on schedule we heard the sound of the motor above the clouds, and then down swooped the big bird to carry us off.

Tramping about on the ice in the rain and cold and struggling against the wind—was it worth it? Here is the list of some of the birds we saw, ten of these having been seen in North America fewer than ten times in the twentieth century: bean goose, white-tailed sea eagle, black-tailed godwit, wood sandpiper, gray-tailed tattler, rufous-necked sandpiper, long-toed stint, red-legged kittiwake, common cuckoo, eyebrowed thrush, dusky thrush, red-throated pipit, bullfinch, and rustic bunting.

In addition, we had good studies of other species that I had seen only infrequently: European wigeon; tufted ducks; harlequins; eiders; surfbirds; ivory gulls; and ancient, marbled, and Kittlitz's murrelets.

Was it worth it? You bet!

A DAY TO REMEMBER ON ATTU ISLAND

May 1977

I am standing in the Aleutian twilight and rain is falling gently on my shoulders. The long arms of the snow-clad mountains above me cradle the mirror-clear cove below, where pairs of eider and flocks of harlequin ducks rock among the harbor's black lava peninsulas. Straw-colored winter grasses quilt the hillside, a somber reminder of the tight grasp of the season, reluctantly releasing slowly melting ice into tiny rivulets that randomly gather into miniature waterfalls and a thousand tundra ponds. Kingfisher Creek and Peaceful River rush into the bay with cascades of gray foam, but along the ocean beach dark green flowerets are emerging like spring gardens. And unlike the drab landscape of the countryside, broken purple mussels, bright rust tide-washed plant clusters, yellow curls of seaweed, vari-colored kelp, and the stark white beaded sea urchin shells create a jagged streamer of color along the dark pebbly beach.

Yesterday the sun broke through the usual gray cloud banks, gracing our blockhouse quarters with a half day of rare brilliant sunshine and sharp shadows. White and black snow buntings flashed against white and black snowfields; rust-collared Lapland longspurs spun to dizzy heights, trilling downward again in spectacular musical display; rock ptarmigan pairs pecked away at new blossoms of dwarf willows along ravines and streams; and the gray-crowned rosy finches sang their low melodies from the black basalt outcroppings. Otherwise, during the past two weeks, the drizzle of rain in the bleak arctic spring alternated with scudding gray clouds and gusty winds, permitting only fair visibility from the hilltops of Murder Point out toward the Bering Sea or into the marsh and bluffs of Massacre Valley.

But another day has ended. The clouds part and a rosy glow gradually spreads over the bay, the background canvas for the delicate etching of shoreline, dwarf willows, and tall grasses.

I am standing in the Aleutian twilight, rain is falling gently on my shoulders, and I am happy.

SPRING COMES TO THE ARCTIC

May 1980

Once again I tug on my Maine hunting boots over thick wool socks, pull the visor of my balaclava down so only my eyes peer out, adjust and securely tie the hood of my waterproof parka, and step outdoors into steadily falling snow. It's time for a five-thirty morning check of the pond, known as Yellow Truck Pond because an abandoned rusty yellow bulldozer hangs atilt on the far edge, thereby distinguishing this small body of water from hundreds of similar tundra ponds. The heat from the small house fades behind me as I softly close the door and deeply breathe in the refreshing cold air. My husband has already disappeared in the direction of the mountain to inspect the ancient archaeological sites known as "the middens," where through the summer months the St. Lawrence Island women and children continue to excavate the layer of dirt above the permafrost, searching for walrus tusk ivory, harpoon handles, bone needles, thread of braided sinew, and many other artifacts formerly used by a Stone Age culture. For the third time we are back home in Gambell, Alaska, on St. Lawrence

Island in the Bering Sea, during the last of the ice breakup in late May, hoping that a west wind will blow rare Asian bird species to our gravelly peninsula.

Gambell has no grass or trees. Walking on the small rounded stones quickly tires our leg muscles. The village huskies begin to bark, signaling to each other that humans have appeared, so beginning their day. Otherwise the land is silent. The native islanders stay up late at night and sleep late into the morning. They keep no work schedules, but they arise each day hoping for a calm ocean so that they can set out in their fiberglass or aluminum boats to hunt walrus, seal, and seabirds for the year's food supply. So except for the canine greetings as I pass the green, red, or yellow prefabricated houses of the village, my world quietly offers only the suppressed excitement of the new day, with hours to explore the frozen lake edge and open patches in the iceberg-mottled sea.

Woodrow and Marie Malewotkuk have taken us into their home for a three-week stay. Before the days of the prefabricated houses, families lived in shacks built of any and all construction material available, from driftwood and lumber collected along the beaches to a few Quonset huts left by the retiring Air Force after World War II. These were known as the old village, which stretched along the waterfront but considerably distant from the ocean's edge, where walrus-skin boats perched in an irregular line balanced upside down on wooden posts. Our family lives in the new village—rows of small wooden houses that arrived on government barges last year.

Woodrow and Marie have five children: Laura, age fifteen; Lena, thirteen; Junior, eleven; Florence, eight; and Chauncey, five, whom we call Malik, his native name. Our house consists of a living room, a small bedroom, and a kitchen on one half of the building, and a bathroom (without fixtures because permafrost underlies the entire island) and two small bedrooms on the other half. A shed encloses the entryway, and here we remove our boots and enter the house in stockinged feet. Here we store the shiny Evinrude motor, an upright freezer, tusks and furs from the hunt, and a new red three-wheeled Honda 70 purchased for Florence and Malik. The Honda 135s, parked outside, provide Laura, Lena, and Junior with transportation, but since it is summer vacation time, they mostly joyride.

From the village to the mountain, along the pebbly shore to the end of the airplane runway and back, the young people of the village race on their Hondas all day long. The big responsibility of Woodrow's children is to keep three five-gallon jugs filled with clear drinking water from the mountain spring. Junior shovels snow to fill a twenty-gallon plastic container parked next to the sink. This we heat for washing dishes and bathing.

My husband and I sleep on a foldout bed in the living room. It has been much used, judging from the broken springs under the thin mattress. Never mind the constant background noise emanating from the television, a new experimental state project that broadcasts only one station, flashing programs I've only heard about. I am introduced to *Benson, Alice, Galactica, The Dukes of Hazzard,* and the nightly two-hour movie. My favorite hour is from five-thirty to six-thirty, when a half hour of Alaska weather forecasts cover the Aleutian Islands to Little Diomede, and we can watch a half hour of live Alaska Senate sessions.

Woodrow and Marie are good to us. We have brought with us freeze-dried food and need only boiling water for our instant oatmeal breakfasts and backpack dinners. Marie keeps a kettle of water boiling over the oil heater all day long for their many cups of tea, so we are no trouble. Otherwise, we eat pilot biscuits with sausage and cheese, Pop-Tarts, instant pudding, and dried fruit. Sitting in the family circle on the kitchen floor, we taste their mukluk (boiled seal), sliced thin and dipped into a bowl of instant mashed potatoes, and it is delicious. Other days they cook frozen chicken in a microwave oven or fry hamburgers over a Coleman camp stove. We heat our Pop-Tarts in their toaster and open cans with their electric can opener. If we did run out of food, we could purchase items in the government store, but its contents are very expensive.

We love our new family. Marie and I talk and laugh, and Marie laughs a lot. Woodrow buys treats: banana-nut bread and big raisin cookies. Some days Laura and Junior take us on a Honda way out to the tundra on the other side of the big lake, and we spend the days climbing the ridges, wading through marshes, following the river, and then returning home by hopping from rock to rock along the shore at the foot of the mountain.

Our family worries about us. One night when we had not returned by dinnertime, they searched through binoculars, and when Woodrow finally spotted our descent from a mountain snowfield, he drove his six-wheeled ATV across tundra, rocks, ravines, and waterways to fetch us home. It was wonderful, after an exhausting day of exploring, to pitch our backpacks into his weird-looking vehicle and bounce like characters in a Walt Disney cartoon back to the village.

Florence sometimes follows me. For hours we walk together, not talking much. She cries with worry when we are late. Every evening we read together: "Little Red Riding Hood" and "The Gingerbread Man." Junior hangs over the back of the sofa where we are sitting and tries to follow the words. Lena likes to sing hymns from a worn hymnbook. Marie, Lena, and I sing "Rock of Ages," "Sweet Hour of Prayer," and "The Church in the Wildwood."

Older men from the village come to visit and talk about the

olden days. Many tales describe peril at sea, or villagers lost on ice floes who survived and made their way back home years later. Old patterns of life are giving way to the new. Marie still stretches seal skins, and she cuts up the walrus and seal meat to hang on outdoor racks to dry for winter. She sews winter parkas for her children out of rabbit skins, worn with the fur on the inside. But they also own down-filled jackets, jeans, and rubber boots.

Every day near the end of our stay we find rare birds along the edge of Yellow Truck Pond or scurrying around in snow patches in the deserted old village: Mongolian plover, common sandpiper, ringed plover, Temminck's stint, and brambling.

The snow and ice are melting rapidly, and it is time to fly in the small bush plane that brought us such a short time ago. Florence cries. Marie hugs me and says, "We not say good-bye. You come back again."

Woodrow says, "This is your home. You are welcome anytime." He puts our packs on a sled, which he will pull behind the six-wheeler. We climb aboard for the short ride, past Yellow Truck Pond, past the old village, to the small sandy airstrip.

The plane arrives. We will come again.

And we did.

THREE VIGNETTES FROM SPRING BIRDING ON ATTU ISLAND

May 1981

The Flapjack Factory

Everybody at Attu camp shared in the household chores. There were pot scrubbers, cook's helpers, a can flattener, runners, kerosene stove tenders, bicycle repairers, and water-fetchers. My husband and I were breakfast pancake-makers, alternating every other day with the oatmeal-and-scrambled-egg crew. The mathematical calculations did not involve computers, but timing was the major factor in flipping one hundred and fifty pancakes on two square griddles on a Coleman camp stove before eight o'clock. So up at six-thirty, bicycle the distance to the upper hut in rain or fog as fast as possible, slice the bacon, mix the milk, open juice and applesauce cans, fill the syrup bottles, and put out cold cereal to appease the appetites of early arrivals. Instant coffee, too.

Then we started cooking thick bacon and nineteen pancake griddle refills. In three weeks of living on Attu Island, nobody came late to breakfast! It was a time of camaraderie around the long tables, a time of eagerness and expectancy of each new day, and as the pot scrubbers took over, for us marvelous freedom for the next forty-eight hours.

The Seawatch

Behind our living quarters on Attu Island rose miles and miles of bluffs that faced the sea. Between us and the bluffs were hills, lakes, and tundra grasses laced with narrow winding streams and marshes, all hiding places for migrating birds in springtime. We could consume a full day in picking our way through the valleys and along the shore with forays up hillsides or into willow thickets.

Nearby was Murder Point, an enormous high grassy bluff that overlooked the ocean. Collapsed Quonset huts, remnants of rusty machinery, and weather-beaten fallen power line poles from World War II days decorated the path to the top. Empty gun emplacement scars, lined with long strands of soft brown grasses, provided protected, comfortable nests from which to spot seabirds.

One by one we discovered the alluring ridge, swinging along, telescopes balanced on our shoulders, settling into a sheltered hole and scanning a scene of wondrous constant motion as we searched the ocean waves and the sky above.

Below us the sharp plumage of the male common eiders polka-dotted the brown mossy shoals. Glaucous-winged gulls, gray-winged white ghosts, giants of their species, ranged high overhead close to shore. Red-faced cormorants, perky crests and bills raised toward the sky, nested on a craggy island directly below us, and as far as the eye could see, they traveled with steady wing-beats between their homes and distant feeding grounds. Small black shapes, buzzing across the water like bumblebees, through the lens of a telescope became tufted puffins. Occasionally a lone common or yellow-billed loon appeared and tantalized the sea-watchers by submerging and reappearing in distant unexpected places. Seals slept on far-off islands, and gray whales breached among whitecaps. Best of all, the call of "Red-legged kittiwake!" or "Jaeger!" or "Shearwater!" rang out as sharp eyes located the moving silhouettes against horizon or cloud or ruffled sea. Even an albatross was possible.

Gradually the Seawatch earned its name—a daily contact between man and the beautiful constant flying forms of the ocean world.

Caps

I pack three wool caps for Attu. A navy-and-red one with a fat pompom on top, which I wear most of the time; a tan balaclava so on windy days I can slide down the soft comfort of the neckband yet have an opening just large enough for my eyes to peer out; and a lightweight Icelandic cloche, which covers my head at night while I am sleeping. Now I know why pioneer women wore nightcaps, and it was not to keep their curlers tucked in!

THE WHITE-TAILED SEA EAGLE
May 1983

I stirred restlessly in my nest of soft grass, stretched, and let my gaze wander to the blue Alaskan sky above me, then back to the rocky pinnacle and the ever-watchful great eagle on her high nest. My companions beside me on the tundra meadow spoke in low voices, but mostly out of respect rather than out of fear of frightening the bird.

On Attu Island in the spring of 1983, a lone birder ranging far from base camp had brought news of the nest of a white-tailed sea eagle, a species normally a resident of Palearctic Europe and Asia. Thus an expectant contingent from our annual three-week campout had set out on the snow-packed mountainous trail to Temnac Valley. We trudged for hours, squinting under the unusual sunshine that coaxed sparkles out of snowdrifts tinged pink from the tiny algae that dwelled below the frozen surface. We clutched a rope that had been fastened to a metal piton at the top of a cliff, swung out over the precipice, descended the sheer cliff to the river below, waded its cold current, followed the shore of black sand, turned into

Temnac Valley, and began the long hike to the eagle's nest.

The first arrivals at the cliff face decided to bivouac on a grassy ridge where they could study the eagle's nest through powerful telescopes, but the site was still terribly far away. So the long-legged striders, including my husband (they ought to form a national organization) forged ahead with the easy great steps striders naturally take.

I followed slowly, not certain about my desire to go the entire distance to the mountain face. My slow steps were contented ones. I really didn't have to catch up with anybody (most days catching up is something I am continually doing), as I had seen white-tailed eagles before, one soaring up Massacre Valley, one circling low over me as I was standing in the yard of upper base, and one high in the sky above me during a previous trip into Temnac Valley. So my sole reason for being here was for this extraordinary view of a rare bird under even rarer circumstances.

A watery channel blocked my progress; it was just too wide for a safe jump to the grassy dike ahead, and there was no helping hand to pull me safely to the other side. Oh well. I pulled my rain pants from my pack, sat down and tugged them on over my boots, tied them tightly with nylon laces, waded across the stream, and then removed them and replaced them in my pack. It was a big nuisance and taxed my patience, but to me, happiness is hiking with dry feet. The leaders, and especially the photographers, were already assembled below the nest, and I thought quite seriously about not continuing by myself. But a little spirit within either pushed or pulled me on. At intervals I stopped for a binocular check to see if the advance party was yet turning back. Eventually I tiptoed up the last tundra hummock and realized my friends had no intention of making this a brief visit. We had not walked all this way to say hi and run.

I was happy to study the great eagle as her fierce gaze moved across the valley and down onto our upturned faces. I was glad I had come to the base of her cliff home. I shivered a little upon the realization that this singular experience was one of the remotest probabilities of my life.

Then the most extreme improbability happened. From the distant sky the male white-tailed sea eagle homed in! He soared in ever decreasing circles until at last he alighted on the high ledge, facing his mate. He had swung in to change the watch. The two proud parents bent over their chick.

I turned to my neighbor and whispered, "I wouldn't have missed this for anything in the world."

With an understanding smile, he answered, "Me neither."

THE LURE OF THE FORK-TAILED SWIFT

May 1986

This tale from Attu Island in the spring of 1986 has a happy ending, so perhaps one can appreciate why we birders keep coming back here.

My husband and I were in a group that worked its way on foot through a snow-filled valley into what we call Massacre Valley, which we had reached by riding our bicycles along a beach road and parking them against a sea wall. Another group of birders combed the beaches, and eventually we met, ate lunch hunched up in grassy hummocks, then separated and started the long walk along the path back to our parked bicycles. At four-fifteen (to be exact) we got word (shouts from birders pedaling bicycles as fast as they could along the nearby waterfront road) that there were two fork-tailed swifts on the other side of the island!

We rushed to get to our bikes, finally reached base camp, and started the trek over the tundra to South Beach. We passed first, second, and third middens and crossed over a very high cliff edge, and reached Krasny Point, a perpendicular rock outcrop that prevented further travel along the shore, which we climbed. We found Pete Isleib waiting there with further directions: two miles over a mountain, down the other side, and over another mountain! (The mountains here are really very high hills.) I could see silhouettes of people climbing toward the top of the first objective, so I started to follow, zigzagging goat-fashion to a saddle where I caught up with a few other Attuvians. Together, we reached the top, only to view another saddle and summit, which we circumvented to the left until we rounded that summit, only to see another peak ahead!

I halted right there, undecided whether to go on or not, when seventy-year-old Dwight Lee panted up the trail behind me and said, "I've been following you. If you can do it, so can I. I've come this far, and I'm not going to stop now." The two of us, now lagging behind the others, had to cross a large snowfield to reach the top of the third summit, and at that point we were looking straight down into a snow-filled valley and another mountain in the distance with antlike figures stretching upward and onward.

I sat down and said, "This is crazy. I'm not going any farther." Our former comrades had already started up the other side.

But Dwight announced stubbornly, "I've come too far to go back now." So we half-skated, half-slid down the mountain and started up the other side. (Many others had had to give up at Krasny, but my husband had insisted I try for it.)

After we reached the snow valley, we met our camp cook on his way back. The good news was that the swifts were still there, and only two more ridges to cross. At this point I was so tired I couldn't even think about the return trip. Then we met two more returnees; they told us to start looking for the swifts as soon as we reached the next snowfield, which we did, and we saw them in the distance. The fifteen or twenty people ahead of us were all sitting around a moon-shaped cliff edge watching the birds swoop overhead. We continued until there was only one snowfield between us and the other birders, but now the swifts were flying right over our heads. Ten minutes later the swifts disappeared to roost for the night! Dwight and I were the last ones to see them.

The journey back was like a bad dream, but we cut off Krasny Point completely and returned to our own valley via a circuitous but more friendly route, aching in every bone and joint. Most of us, in order to climb more easily, had dropped backpacks along the way; I knew I could find mine some other day. My hair was wet from perspiration. My wool cap was in my backpack and I didn't have gloves. In the cold night air I was chilled to the bone.

As we neared base camp it was almost midnight. Everyone had waited in the dining room for news. My husband brought me a plate of hot spaghetti and a cup of cider. I ate the welcome meal like a zombie, then left for our room at lower base, where I found the warmth of our little heater and a big can of hot water for a bath.

The following morning my husband and the rest of the birders went to look for the swifts, starting out fresh and taking a shorter route. Meanwhile, a red-breasted flycatcher showed up on the airplane runway, so instead of resting I spent the whole morning chasing it.

So goes life on Attu Island!

PART IV

NARROW ESCAPES

A GREEK ARMY SCARE

May 1967

The afternoon was sunny and warm that quiet Sunday in Komotini in northern Greece as eight dedicated birders set out by bus to search for a large hawk, a honey buzzard, in the mountainous region near the border with Bulgaria.

On the narrow, twisting road, our vehicle crawled around hairpin turns while our eyes were fastened on the background of blue sky and white clouds. Then on shifting thermals a honey buzzard sailed into view, and the bus stopped abruptly. Grabbing binoculars and cameras, we eager birders spread out over the mountain.

Not all of our birding group on the First Ornithological of Greece had joined our party, as they preferred an afternoon of rest after our early-morning strenuous days afield. The tour was led by John Santikos, a young Greek man who had grown up in Texas, who had returned to live in Athens and manage with his brother a real estate business left to them by their recently deceased father. John had watched his countrymen shoot birds for sport, and he didn't like it. So he decided to organize a birding tour whose publicity might make the public aware of the plight of the birds and the long-term effects of hunting on the nation's ecology.

He attracted such names as Roger Tory Peterson, noted author of the Peterson Field Guide series; Carl Buchheister, president of the National Audubon Society, and his wife, Harriet, a noted botanist; Stuart Keith, head of the ornithology department at the American Museum of Natural History in New York; and Alta Niebuhr, author of *The Herbs of Greece* and an avid birder. Plus a few less-illustrious figures such as ourselves: a small-town lawyer and his schoolteacher wife, who were just excited to be there.

I had just erected my spotting scope and was peering through it into the vast panorama of mountaintops in the distance, when a Greek army unit surrounded by snarling dogs came marching up the road, shouting incomprehensible Greek words—but there was no doubt about their meaning. From our various positions at the edge of the rock-strewn road, we hurried back to the bus. The soldiers threw rocks at the leaping, barking dogs—no resemblance to the well-trained United States Army's K-9 Corps! As the last birder boarded the bus, the soldiers, shouldering rifles, filed in after us.

We had accidentally infiltrated the three-mile buffer zone between Greece and Bulgaria! In joining our search for the big hawk, our driver had completely missed the roadside warning sign that forbade entrance into this no-man's land.

Unfortunately, this was also just a week after the young king had been put under house arrest. Tanks patrolled the city streets; riflemen stood guard on rooftop corners of tall buildings. This was not the time to involve United States personnel in a suspicious activity, and we had with us our nation's commercial attaché, our immigration attaché, and the head of the U.S.-directed YMCA. The men in our group who spoke fluent Greek remained silent.

Our driver was directed to drive us to a border patrol station, where the soldiers ordered him to enter a cavernous wooden building. He was interrogated for an hour and repeatedly assured the army captain in charge that we were a harmless group of people who had assembled in Greece to watch birds. Apparently the captain did not believe him, because finally we were all summoned inside, where we climbed an unpainted wooden stairway and arrived in a large, bare, high-ceilinged room that contained only a desk and a single lightbulb dangling from the ceiling. Behind the desk glowered an officer whose uniformed chest was covered with colorful campaign ribbons.

The captain collected all the cameras and pulled out the exposed film. Then he ordered us to sign our names on a sheet of paper. At that moment I almost panicked, fearful that as the only woman present I might be separated from my friends, at least overnight. Looking back, my presence may have saved the situation as the captain looked down on a very small woman wearing gray-green army fatigues and a soiled white sailor's cap. Maybe he chuckled to himself. Such a motley crew could not be international spies! Anyway, after four hours of questioning and detention, we were sent back to the state-owned Xenia Hotel still accompanied by a contingent of soldiers carrying machine guns.

The following morning a summons came for my husband. Instead of signing his name on the sheet of paper the night before, he had handed over a business card, which had indicated to them that he was our leader. (And probably his name was the only name the officers could easily read.) The captain was waiting for him in the hotel lobby, and he expressed regret at our treatment at the border. He had confirmed the fact that a birding tour really existed and said that if we ever returned, to please call upon him and he would escort us wherever we wanted to go.

A satisfactory ending to what began as a quiet Sunday afternoon!

BABY BARN OWLS

August 1979

I do not ordinarily risk my life to see a bird. Once, when my husband and I were backpacking in Alaska, the edge of a cliff crumbled away underneath our feet, and we desperately clung to alder roots and wriggled through them on our stomachs. Then we constructed an alder root ladder and dropped a horribly long way to the beach below, where at high tide a skiff could get in to pick us up.

Small wonder, then, that I found myself staring with apprehension at a ladder leading to a loft in a ramshackle abandoned barn near Vancouver, British Columbia, where my husband had discovered a nest of baby barn owls. He needed someone to hold the flash unit for his camera, and I was the only someone for miles around. Besides, I had never seen a baby barn owl.

The ladder's top rung was recessed, which left an enormous vacant space to jump over to gain access to the loft. I could only hook my arms around the wooden supports, give a mighty heave, and hoist myself to the upper story, much the way one hoists oneself into a boat. I did it, forcing from my thoughts the further dangers of the return descent.

We stood up and surveyed our surroundings. I had forgotten the dizzying heights of a barn loft; as a child I had fearlessly swung on a rope and flung myself into the deep, fragrant piles of hay. This loft floor was bare of hay and strewn with generations of owl pellets. Openings at each end and occasional broken wallboards provided easy entry and departure routes for the adult owls. And at one end, on a high wooden shelf, four infant barn owls in white woolly sleepers glared down at two two-legged animals with enormous protruding eyes, and in unison they hissed ferociously, undoubtedly strengthening their lungs for chilling screams in later life.

Most baby animals appeal to our tender instincts. These babies were ugly. I'll admit, though, they did have personality. One was obviously older and protective of his smaller brothers and sisters. As a family unit they defended their home. We snapped our photos and retreated.

We reversed the procedure over the yawning aperture, took a last look at the abandoned barn, and for the first time noticed an enormous white board on which someone had painted in bold black letters: TRESPASSERS AND VIOLATORS WILL BE KILLED!

GABON AIRPORT

September 1987

We left Lusaka, Zambia, and were on our way to the Lutheran mission in Cameroon for a three-month stay. Our evening flight was destined for Paris, so we had to overnight in Libreville, the capital of Gabon, where we would connect with a morning flight to Douala, Cameroon. If we could show that we had an an ongoing ticket, we would not need a visa for an overnight stay. As we deplaned at nine o'clock, we crossed the distance from the aircraft to the shabby, unpainted room that was the customs office, on a night that was completely black and starless.

We were the only passengers to leave the plane in Libreville. The lone officer on duty spoke only French. When we explained that we were in transit, he stamped our passports, put them in a drawer, and told us we could get them in the morning.

After we had claimed our luggage in an equally squalid room next door, we were surrounded by a number of young men trying to grab our suitcases. When I asked for a taxi, the man nearest to me maneuvered us out to the street where his friend waited in a battered old car, and after I explained that we did not have any local currency, they said they would drive us to the hotel and wait, which they did. My husband cashed a traveler's check at the hotel desk, paid them, and asked them to take us back to the airport in the morning. I had little faith in their promises.

Our room at the Okoume Palace Intercontinental was lovely, though we had little time to enjoy its comfort. We breakfasted on a patio overlooking the ocean, and that is all I remember about Gabon. As they had promised, the boys returned to take us to the airport, where we arrived at eight o'clock, two hours before our scheduled departure.

A seething mass of humanity, all pushing and jostling in line, shoved us around, and when my husband finally reached the head of the line (by doing some necessary pushing himself), the travelers continued to hand tickets rudely over his shoulder to the agent behind the counter. We got our boarding passes and checked our luggage.

In the midst of a terrific din of voices, I explained to the ticket agent that our passports had been kept overnight. (I'd practiced the sentences while trying to get to sleep the night before.) The first time through I drew a blank stare; the second time I tried, his eyes lit up in understanding and he said the word "polizei" and pointed to a sign over the departure door.

The customs line for checking passports also said POLIZEI, so we stood in line. When I gave the same explanation to the control officer, he turned to another person behind the desk, who left to fetch our passports. Time went by while dozens of people streamed by. It was after nine o'clock and I realized we were running out of time.

I noticed three uniformed officers standing in a back room, just standing. I walked up to one of them and asked, "Parlez-vouz anglais?" He shook his head. So I made my request in four words, "Passport. Polizei. Dernier soir." He patted my shoulder and said to come, and I followed him out of the departure lounge onto the tarmac and almost ran down to the door of the arrival lounge we had entered the night before.

The police office was empty and locked! My guide placed his hands on my shoulders, pressed me firmly, and announced that he would come back. He took off. I stared into the empty office. He returned with a large policewoman, who unlocked the door. On a shelf behind the desk was a stack of dozens of passports, but ours were not among them. My heart sank and time was flying by. It was steaming hot in there. The policewoman began opening desk drawers. From the last bottom drawer she pulled out two passports—ours.

I said, "Merci beaucoup!" and grabbed them and ran. I found the airstrip. But a soldier was guarding the exit door and refused to let me enter. I grabbed a passing worker and explained what had happened; then after a short conversation the guard unlocked the door and let me in.

Now I was going against the traffic. Each passenger had to go through a curtained-off room for hand-baggage inspection, ladies and men separately. With authority I pulled aside the curtains, brushed past the startled authorities, and ran the reverse path to the passport control desk and handed the passports to my husband. Our papers were stamped, and at the baggage inspection room they waved us through. We just made it!

But my story isn't over yet. On arriving in Douala, two of our bags were missing, mine with all my clothing for three months at the mission, and my husband's camera equipment, which he usually carried on board as hand luggage. The porters searched everywhere, but no luck. So we filled out the proper forms. We were informed that the plane had gone on to another destination but would return at three o'clock, and please would we return, and possibly our bags would be found.

At three o'clock we returned to the airport and waited for the plane, which did not arrive until after four—and no luggage. When the carousel stopped moving, my husband went back to the claim office. A new man offered to send a Telex to Libreville, but, remembering the pandemonium of the morning, that didn't offer us much consolation.

We made a plan. My husband would return to the airport the next morning and once again look for our luggage, and I would go to a store and buy a skirt and a couple of blouses. I didn't dare go to Ngaoundere without a change of clothes.

I was dining alone at breakfast when a lovely-looking lady sat near me, also eating alone. I related my problem and asked where I should go shopping. "Only one place," she answered: "Mono-Prix."

The supermarket's merchandise was awful, with very little in the way of clothing, poor quality, and no small sizes. I wandered along the racks of dresses and finally found a sleeveless, drawstring-waist turquoise shift that hung down to my ankles. I tried it on in a small room crowded with hardware supplies and decided I could sew it up the sides.

Outside, the streets were traditionally native with venders, blocks of used clothing, food stalls, traffic jams, and people striding everywhere. Fortunately, I found a uniformed traffic controller and he stopped a taxi for me.

It was still only eleven-thirty and I was certain my husband would not be back from the airport. Yet our room key was not at the desk. So I rode up on the elevator hugging my packages and opened the unlocked door. My husband shouted, "Happy birthday!" and pointed to our missing pieces of baggage with RUSH signs pasted all over them. And it was September seventeenth! My sixty-eighth birthday.

DISASTER IN ZAMBIA

October 1988

The picture of our private monthlong three-person birding tour in Zambia is a collage of living luxuriously in castles with servants who do everything, from carrying luggage, turning down beds, serving drinks and tea, and even washing pajamas if they are left on the bed, to handling disastrous breakdowns of support systems. My husband; my birding friend Phoebe Snetsinger; our Welsh guide, Bob Sternstjedt; and I had hired a safari company to provide us with tents, food, and transportation. The following report will explain the title of this story.

A very rare heron, the shoebill stork, dwells among the papyrus reeds in the Banguela Swamp in the heart of Africa. This was our highest priority, so after a day spent repacking our equipment, we started off in a Land Rover driven by a local young man named Thomas. We left Zambia's one paved highway for a narrow dirt road that angled across cassava fields and through scattered villages, and here disaster struck. A wheel came off our Land Rover! We were left stranded, surrounded by a few bamboo and grass huts and staring natives, who came from miles around.

The safari season had ended, so no lifesaving vehicles came along to rescue us. At the Banguela Swamp, still about ten miles away, supposedly a crew with a truck and food waited for us. We asked the village chief if anybody had a bicycle we could borrow. The village was too poor, and he answered no. We carried only a small supply of peanut butter and bread and a few packets of instant oatmeal for emergencies. And this was an emergency! The natives had no food to offer. Thomas brought water from a lagoon covered with scum, boiled it, and added iodine tablets. In hot Africa, water is all-important. Amazingly, we did not get sick.

Night came, and finally the onlookers drifted away. We spread sheets of plastic alongside the road and tried to sleep under the brilliant starry sky. At midnight the temperature dropped, and we had only our raincoats for cover. At four o'clock we were so uncomfortable that we still had not fallen asleep, so we got up and drank cups of hot coffee.

A young boy came along, pedaling a bicycle loaded with bunches of bananas. But the bicycle belonged to his employer, and he did not dare part with it. Finally we bribed him with fifteen dollars, a month's wage in Zambia, and a promise to return his wheels.

Our guide, Bob, who was suffering from a bout of malaria, began cycling toward the crew waiting for us near the papyrus beds. As he told us later, after several miles of pedaling he encountered some natives and, too exhausted to continue himself, sent one of them on with a message to send the truck for us. At noon the truck arrived. We left Thomas and one of the crew to guard the Land Rover, and we drove the last few miles into the swamp. Here we found an open-sided cabin, where our cook was squatting over an open fire, preparing food. And as we surveyed the tall reeds in the swamp around us, we saw two shoebill storks right out in the open! We had prepared ourselves to paddle about for hours searching for them.

We sent the truck with food back to Thomas, but the truck broke down and never returned! We were now miles from nowhere and without transportation. No phones. No wireless. No traffic. I noticed a bicycle parked against a wall of the cabin and asked if one of the natives could ride out for help. Actually, there was a hunting camp nearby and we hoped they would have wireless communication, so we sent one of our native cooks over with a request for help. The camp was closed for the season, but our emissary returned with a dilapidated Land Cruiser with a battery so low that the natives had to push the vehicle to get it started. We piled into the small compartment in the rear and returned to the waiting Thomas and the derailed Land Rover.

Now we siphoned the gas from our abandoned vehicle and began the return journey along the narrow road until darkness fell. Without auto lights we drove along the winding forest road in the light of the beam of a handheld flashlight. We finally reached the safari headquarters, and a half hour later we sat down to a three-course dinner under the chandeliers of the spacious dining room.

Of course nobody in Africa should start out on safari with only one vehicle. But with support trucks carrying tents and food, the next morning we departed in high spirits. Too soon another disaster awaited us. In driving across Zambia, travelers are stopped many times by police patrols at checkpoints. At one such checkpoint a message awaited us that one of our support vehices had gone off to a nearby town for wheel repairs. A little later we came upon our stranded support truck, which had two flat tires and no repair kit!

We transferred the food from the truck to the roof of our vehicle and proceeded to our destination, a national forestry cabin in a small town, where at dark the truck finally arrived. The crew placed cots in a one-room mud hut and cooked dinner over a charcoal fire. Dinner at eight, the English custom. And our servers insisted on setting up a table under the trees, covering it with a linen cloth, and serving the soup course first!

Our next target was in northwest Zambia, a four-hundred-kilometer drive to our first stop at Greystone, a completely self-sufficient farm. The family lived in a manor surrounded by several small homes, and they had their own coffee plantation, cattle, chickens, and vegetable gardens, and lots of mechanical equipment. They were wealthy landowners in the midst of the usual thatched-roof hut community of African families composed of ten or twelve poorly clothed children.

Our support vehicle (a truck pulling a trailer with tents, etc.) had gone ahead to prepare our meals at the farm, but it never arrived because the crew had to remain overnight at a midway village, as they couldn't get any diesel fuel until the next morning. We were rescued by an invitation to join the family at dinner. The following morning, at breakfast, again we were their guests.

Our truck still did not come. After we had birded all day along a winding creek and were still without resources, this really sympathetic family included the five of us at dinner, which was cooked by an elderly African chef and served with wine and the cook's specialty, mulberry torte. Saved again!

The supply truck arrived the following morning, and we continued on another long drive to the Mwinilunga area in northwest Zambia. Here was a different habitat with different bird species, and the camping equipment was supposed to go ahead of us. We birded in woodlands along the way, but when we arrived at our proposed site, there were no tents or vehicles!

While we sat pondering our fate in the fading twilight, the truck finally arrived and the crew hurried to set up camp, but it was difficult in the dark. They erected two large tents, connected lights to the Land Rover's battery, and dug a latrine (placing a bamboo shelter around it) while the head cook got to work providing dinner. The men had discovered that I loved the dark, sticky wild honey, and they always put out a piece of tree bark filled with the thick, sweet syrup, which I ate with my fingers. A tarp supported by poles created a dining room, and under it were placed a card table and chairs, and eventually dinner was ready to be served. Bob had to sleep under the tarp, but the next day the men erected a tent for him and put up a shower barrel inside a bamboo wall.

During the following night, rain suddenly poured down in torrents. I was lying on my cot, enjoying the sound of rain on the roof, until I heard a sloshing around us at midnight. Only half of our tent roof had been covered with a tarp, and my half had rain streaming in! My clothing, binoculars, and everything else on the floor were soaking wet. Fortunately, our backpacks were on high ground. It was difficult to go back to sleep after rescuing our equipment, so we had a rather sleepless night and arose at four o'clock as usual, to be birding at daylight. I hung out my wet things on bushes, and gradually, over the next day and a half, my clothes dried out.

Next we set out for the Nyika Plateau in the country of Malawi. After a long drive, struggling up over mountain roads, long after dark and in the rain, we signed in at an army patrol unit. During our five days on the Nyika Plateau we did not need a support crew. We had brought our own food supply, and the cook in residence prepared dinner for us. Our dependable driver, Thomas, saw to it that we had breakfast along the trail after our five o'clock start, and he served hot coffee, bread, and cheese. We ate cabbage salad, oranges, and bananas for lunch. We returned from the long hikes, ate dinner, wrote up our field notes, and tumbled into bed.

A slight problem occurred as we attempted to leave the country. In Malawi, women are not allowed to wear trousers, and we were told we would not be allowed to cross the border wearing jeans. One solution would be to drive into the village and purchase the six yards of cloth necessary to wrap around us as the native women did, but as luck would have it, I had packed a lightweight army-green cotton shirtwaist and, in addition, a wraparound skirt. Phoebe and I donned them using the forest as a dressing room, and we passed inspection at the customs gate.

After our descent from Malawi, our next stop was a guest cottage near hot springs. Everybody else had enjoyed the hot springs during the day, but I had remained out birding late, and only flickering lights from the camp guided my steps home. So after dark I lay alone in the steamy bubbles for half an hour, and every bit of tiredness and tension melted away.

We broke camp and started for the Zaire (formerly Belgian Congo) border but insisted on taking along a tent, just in case. We had been slow learners. That night, predictably, our support truck did not arrive.

We had to consult the village chief for permission to camp on his land. He was very kind and led us to an isolated area, where Thomas chopped a small clearing alongside some vague tracks we had followed. Thomas erected the tent, which barely held our three cots. Bob and Thomas slept under a tarp connected to the Land Rover by two tall stakes that Thomas had cut from the forest. Then Thomas cooked some rice and added it to the only food we carried—instant soup. We had purchased a fresh pineapple along the way, the sweetest in the world. Luckily, it didn't rain and we had one of our best slumbers in Zambia.

The next morning we ate cold rice and pineapple for breakfast. We had passed many small communities along the way but had had no opportunity to obtain food from the natives, as they came begging from us. The only other staple we could buy was a giant mushroom the size of a small umbrella, which grows only in certain damp conditions near the roots of forest trees. Few and far between, but a cash crop for a boy or girl who happens to find one.

All the time during the monthlong safari, we were seeing wonderful new birds, following trails in the forest, crossing small streams on slippery logs. By nightfall we were really tired and ready to fall onto our cots. The weather was mild, mornings refreshing and noons hot.

At last we began the return trip toward Lusaka, and our first overnight stay was at a mission rest house, a sturdy building near a river, surrounded by small cottages, a central dining building, and a separate kitchen, where for the first time our crew arrived on time and cooked dinner. They had had to abandon the trailer, as the hitch had become irreparably broken. We hadn't had bread for sandwiches for days, so our cook baked a loaf of whole wheat bread, which was delicious!

Our last driving day returned us to the farm, where our support truck never did arrive. The family had left for England, but orders had been left for the cook to prepare dinner for us. Again it was a memorable meal, with stuffed duckling, salads, fresh veggies, and this time, gooseberry torte.

At three-thirty in the morning on our final day, we arrived in

Ndola for a try for just one more bird. We had expected to have oatmeal for breakfast, but there was no sign of our crew, so we made a pot of tea and Thomas produced a plastic bowl containing cold boiled potatoes.

The surprising thing about our month in Zambia, in spite of the breakdowns of our support system, is that we laughed our way through it all, maintained our health, and remember our adventures with nostalgia. What would we have done without Thomas? It could never happen again!

JUNGLAVEN

February 1996

I originally thought there would not be much to recount about the trip my husband and I took to Junglaven, Venezuela, a remote fishing camp on a tributary of the Orinoco River, but here occurred two of the most bizarre incidents of my life. From Caracas we flew over the rain forest for an hour in a light six-seated air taxi and landed on a grass runway about five miles from the camp. A decrepit truck, barely held together by exposed bolts and wires, carried us on a narrow dirt road created by many traverses of said truck. From the road's edge, six trails about a mile apart had been cut into the forest. Outside the vast forest lay open savannah occasionally dotted with stands of small trees and bushes. A lagoon, linked to a river, flowed in front of our cabin. In these habitats we spent two weeks of birding for such neotropical species as toucans, aracaris, parrots, puffbirds, jacamars, and other jungle species.

At the end of the first week, as the other participants in our group left the camp to return home, my husband and I accompanied them to the grass airplane taxiway and waved good-bye, and on our return to camp three black curassows ran along in front of the truck for several turns in the road. Our friends missed them by minutes! The next day seven gray-winged trumpeters did the same thing, finally veering off and away into the forest. Just the luck of the day.

On my second day of birding alone, on Trail #2, I flushed a pair of marbled wood quail, whose camouflaged feathers matched the leaf-strewn path but who appeared gold as they flew through a shaft of sunlight.

Perhaps the most satisfying views of a special bird happened when Lorenzo, the camp handyman and truck driver, took my husband with his camera on the big river while I spent the morning on the savannah. At about noon, when the truck had not reappeared and I did not want to sit waiting on the thatch-canopied wooden bench at the little grass airstrip, though tired and hot I decided to walk to meet the truck. Just after passing the fishing camp, as I was about to start down the hill to the road that led to the boat landing, a sunbittern flew into a small pool of water that had collected in the road during a recent rainstorm. For at least ten minutes I watched, entranced, using both binoculars and scope, though I was almost too close for that. The sunbittern raised its coppery wings and delicately stalked around in the pool. There was no way I could have intercepted the truck as it roared into camp, and the beautiful big bird flew away.

The third day of our protracted stay was so beautiful that I asked Lorenzo to drop me off at Trail #3, about three miles from camp, as he was driving to another fishing camp to get help to repair his truck. He would return in late afternoon and pick me up somewhere along the road. This was the first time I had carried no umbrella, raincoat, or even water canteen. I loved to walk free in the forest, and although the trail did not produce the rufous-winged cuckoo I had hoped for, I was having a lovely time.

I followed the trail, which led back to the road, as the sky darkened and threatened rain. I wasn't worried, as this had occurred many afternoons. But I looked around for two large banana leaves, and, after checking them for ants and spiders, used them to keep my head dry. I then laid my field cap over the lens of my telescope. What I did not expect was a sudden fierce storm of such intensity that branches began to fall around me and the truck tracks became a rushing flood of brown water. Lightning flashed and thunder roared. I still stood, unworried, watching for the truck to arrive, until I realized it probably wouldn't even start in such weather. The sky darkened even more, and crashing sounds echoed through the evening air.

I did not want to be caught in the forest after dark and had to decide what to do. I decided to walk back to camp. As I looked for safe footing on either side of the road or in the slightly elevated center grassy strip, I lectured myself: "Be careful. Don't be stupid and break a leg. You'll be fine."

That was before I encountered the first large tree felled across the road. Fortunately, it was still light enough to see, and I could make my way around the enormous root end. I regained the trail. A river of water surged ahead of me, and I was thankful I had started for the camp, since the truck would be blocked until someone could saw an opening in the tree. As I trudged along in the pouring rain, having lost my banana-leaf hat, the thunder and lightning continued to crack overhead, the world became dark, and it seemed that I was on some other planet—an eerie feeling. Finding firm ground along the edges of the now almost submerged track was difficult.

Then I arrived at the second downed tree, and this one I

could not walk around. The roots were too large for me to climb over, but I tackled the leafy end, climbing under and over the huge branches until I emerged on the other side. I looked down and saw that my tan field pants were in tatters.

I sang to myself as I trudged along in the mud. Somehow I missed seeing the marker for Trail #2, but when I arrived at the opening to a banana plantation, I was in familiar territory and knew that Junglaven was only a half hour away.

I had been walking for three hours, and it must have been about nine o'clock when through the trees I saw the welcoming lights of the lodge and ran into my last obstacle: a tree that had blown down right across the entrance to our cabin. Suddenly I heard a tremendous cracking noise as a huge tree crashed onto the roof of the lodge but, surprisingly, did not break through. I cut across the lawn to the lodge and the smell of our cook's hot soup and to a husband who hadn't worried because all that time he had thought I was with Lorenzo.

About ten-thirty that night a jeep from the other camp drove in with several men who had come along to help clear the road. Lorenzo's truck had had a flat tire as he'd started out to rescue me, so he had walked back to the other camp for help. At the fallen tree barriers they broke the trees down by ramming them with the jeep, then dragging broken pieces aside just enough to allow the jeep to pass through. When they found that I was safely at home, the grins on their faces were marvelous to see. They probably thought I had been eaten by a jaguar! The next morning Lorenzo picked up my scope, unharmed where I had parked it. Unbelievably, the tracks were almost dry again.

The storm was not the final trauma of our stay at Junglaven. I often get nicked on my legs as I walk along woodland trails, arriving home after a birding trip with little scabs that last for a week or two, so I was not perturbed by a small scab on the back of my leg. After departing from Venezuela, we drove to the Davis Mountains of western Texas for a few additional days of warmth before returning to our freezing Michigan weather, and when I finally decided to remove the scab, I discovered, holding it in the palm of my hand, that the scab had legs. I knew right away that it was a tick, but I was in shock as I went to bed, and I had a sleepless night.

Professor Harlan Thorvilson of Texas Tech University's Plant and Soil Science Department identified my little friend as an engorged female tick. Dr. Robert Kimbrouogh of the university's Department of Infectious Diseases advised me to watch for symptoms such as swollen lymph glands, and he told me to send the specimen to our state public health lab for further identification.

And that is how one female *Amblyomma oblongoguttatum* came to reside in a bottle as RML, 122352 in the National Tick Collection of the Centers for Disease Control in Atlanta, Georgia. And I was still an enthusiastic seventy-six-year-old birder.

PART V

THE AMAZON

THE AMAZON RIVER IN PERU

January 1984

Who has not dreamed of sailing down the Amazon, where the sun beats down unmercilessly, monkeys swing through the jungle trees, parrots raucously shriek overhead, and piranha lurk in shallow waters?

My husband and I did just that, and the picture is quite true, although the Amazon is such a wide river that only its tributaries are narrow enough to provide an arched roof of impenetrable forest leaves.

A palm-thatch roof covered the transport canoe that carried us in five hours from Iquitos, Peru's largest inland city, to Explorama Lodge, a group of thatch-roofed cabins constructed in a small clearing on a bluff near the Amazon's headwaters. No docks eased our embarking; shouldering backpacks and pushing luggage ahead of us, we wriggled on as best we could. Everywhere were muddy riverbanks. At first we kept close to shore. We saw huts, fields, dugout canoes, children playing, and women washing clothes at the water's edge—all the activities of a native Peruvian civilization. Sometimes the Amazon was so wide we could hardly see the opposite shore. We passed islands and floating trees, steep bluffs and dense forest.

As we neared our inlet, precariously juggling our luggage we were forced to abandon the big canoe for a smaller one that proceeded up a narrow, winding channel to the Explorama dock.

Tucked into the jungle, adjoining rooms in groups of four set on stilts and connected by thatched walkways had been constructed of thin slats. Each room contained a cot (mosquito netting tucked in all around), a basin and water pitcher (a set of written instructions informed us to "pull curtain and throw out wash water, being careful no one is passing underneath"), and a short drape that could be pulled shut to enclose the open side. The floor slats of the adjacent shower building were spaced so far apart that for the first few days I feared becoming dizzy if I peered through them to the ground below.

On arrival we were too excited to unpack, and even though afternoon is not the optimal time for birding, we immediately investigated the first of many jungle trails that were to become very familiar. As we started out, our first new bird appeared in a tree within sight of the cabins—a speckled spinetail. Our group of birders filed quietly along the cool shadowed pathway that turned and twisted until it wound up into a high forest. Here we were rewarded with a good view of a scale-backed antbird, the first of more than thirty species of antbirds we would identify. At dinnertime we served ourselves from a buffet that offered fish, rice, and many kinds of vegetables and fruit.

Had not the day been long enough? Did anybody want to go "owling"? Of course we did! Stars twinkled in the black sky, fireflies flashed their tiny lights all around, and only the soft shadows of our comrades betrayed our invasion of the dark forest. Clustered together in anticipation, we listened as Ted Parker, our guide, played a tape of the call of the crested owl. Right away from deep in the jungle came a soft answer, then a whirring flight of feathers. A giant shape landed on a tree limb high above us. The owl had enormous earlike tufts, clearly displayed in the light of our beacons. Our first day in the jungle had come to a spectacular close!

Life on the Amazon fell into a pattern. Breakfast was at five o'clock, the magic time when life in the jungle begins to stir, birds begin to chatter, cool air invigorates. The daily search for new neotropical bird species led us through the river's floodplain, an area of special kinds of plants and special bird life, up to the high forest, where in an opening against the sky, treetops heavy with fruit attracted brilliantly colored tanagers: green and gold, paradise, turquoise, and opal-crowned. Flocks of parrots and parakeets squawked across the sky. A spangled cotinga reflected the morning's gold sunshine. Toucans snapped their tremendous bills. And always we listened for flocks of the wary antbirds.

Just as we began to really feel at home, it was time to climb back into the canoe for a trip farther up the Amazon to the Napo River. At the confluence of these two rivers begins the Amazon's three-thousand-mile run to the Atlantic Ocean.

At ExplorNapo Lodge merely an open veranda built on stilts became our lodging. We slept on mattresses placed in rows on the floor, each enclosed with a rectangle of mosquito netting suspended from overhead. Chairs had been carved from logs and surrounded the long wooden table—an all-purpose piece of furniture used for dining and as a work table. Stairs haphazardly cut out of tree trunks provided the precarious footing for the journey from the lodge to the latrines and showers at ground level. But we loved it. There was coffee and bread and jam to eat at dawn. There were morning hours on jungle trails, canoe rides to river islands, and afternoon walks to the shore after the careful crossing of a bridge that had been built of logs laid side by side. We identified more than a hundred new bird species, from the tiny sapphire-spangled emerald hummingbird to the disheveled, helter-skelter hoatzins. But one of the best sightings was a lanceolated monklet discovered by my husband after everybody else had passed it by. Fortunately, monklets stay put for a long, long time.

Our three weeks on the Amazon River came to an end one day, and we reboarded the big canoe. Small clearings, thatched-roof huts, children waving from shore, clumps of mud sliding into the waterways, crecopias and vine tangles—all passed in review.

During our jungle stay we had grown accustomed to the moldy odor that accompanied our damp clothing and our leather boots. Nothing ever dried out. So back to civilization and a real motel, where we all washed our clothes and spread everything out in the sun to dry, completely covering the lawn furniture and ornamental shrubs, probably to the dismay of the motel staff. And while the laundry was drying, we all went out to sea. And *that* is another story!

EXPLORER'S INN, PERU

February 1984

As far as the airlines are concerned, Puerto Maldonado is the end of the earth. From that jungle village only waterways stretch out for transportation into the largest river system in the world.

Since we now were veteran Amazonian travelers, our four-hour boat ride up the Tambopata River to the Explorer's Inn was a relaxing affair. Let the tourists exclaim in dismay over the muddy shore and tricky leap to the canoe's bow; let them marvel at the primitive scene along the shore—dugouts roofed with thatch and loaded down with too many people, toddlers allowed to paddle about in shallow boats, macaws flapping and chattering treetop high. But underneath my sophisticated nonchalance I truly never tired of the scenes.

Our inn complex had four thatched-roof buildings, each composed of four rooms walled with slats so thin one could almost see through them. Candles (set in untippable cross-sections of small tree trunks) furnished all the light we needed. And we had the luxury of our own running water, albeit cold.

Similar candlelight on the dining table illuminated our predawn breakfasts. For three hours every evening a generator furnished electricity. We had more comfort than we needed. We could recline in the canvas chairs on our veranda and watch the world go by: the staff weaving new thatch for roofs, a yardman cutting grass in the clearing with a scythe, scarlet macaws crossing the sky with raucous coughs, the brilliant orange-and-black troupial singing gaily as he wove his dangling basketlike nest, and the evening's antics of the Cuvier's toucan.

We had arrived at the Explorer's Inn during the rainy season. Looking back, I sometimes think we were preoccupied more with the disastrous trails than with the birds. Every bit of trail in the low forest was either muddy or filled with water deep enough to warrant log ramps—two or three small logs hastily thrown together, the one in the middle usually rather wobbly, which required considerable balance to traverse. Not a mere dozen, but thirty or forty such impedimentia frequently halted any rapid progress we hoped to make along the main trail, which covered one and a half miles along low land and rose gradually one and a half more miles and ended at Big Lake. There were also seven bridges over major forest streams, which were usually four rather large logs, sometimes actually fastened together with pieces of wire. All but two had railings that consisted of a sapling laid in two notched sticks that had been jammed onto each shore, plus one in the middle. Compared to slip-sliding over the interminable little bridges with muddy boots, we viewed the big bridges as secure superstructures. Anyway, we became used to the obstacle course and after a few days thought nothing of it.

It was always easy to get an early start in the jungle. Candlelight cast a warm glow as the boys brought papaya, pancakes with marmalade, or fresh bread (when the cook had enough flour), and sometimes an egg. Good coffee. Then we would pull a couple of bananas from one of the bunches hanging about, slip rain gear onto our belts, and start up the trail. There were so many bird songs we did not recognize that we would record one on tape and play it back, and often a small bird would appear, restlessly flitting through bushes and tangled vines and usually managing to conceal itself behind the thickest leaves. Often identification was made more difficult by the dim light. But thus we found great and bluish-gray antshrikes; streaked antwren; and warbling, white-flanked, and white-browed antbirds.

One morning a razor-billed curassow (black, two and a half feet high, bright red knob above the bill) stood directly in our path. Another day a gray-necked woodrail walked in front of us. Black-tailed trogons and rufous motmots perched noiselessly. A pair of jacamars chased each other and landed on a branch over our heads. We followed the call of a screaming piha and found a nondescript little gray bird screaming his head off only ten feet off the ground. We would stop to watch teddy-bear-shaped tamarind monkeys and sweet-faced capuchins fling themselves from tree to tree, performing really audacious aerial acrobatics. Another frequent sound in the jungle was the crash of falling Brazil nuts, tremendous nuts with a shell so thick and tough that only a machete in the hands of a skilled native could cut it open.

Floating in a canoe out on Big Lake, we startled the horned screamers and hoatzins. Even a ladder-tailed nightjar, blending its sand color into the dead palm fronds, woke up and flew along the shore. We fished for small piranha with string and hook tied to a stick, using pieces of meat for bait. I finally caught one and it was bright yellow and reminded me of a sunfish. I held it gently and released it back into the water.

The blue morph, fluttering like a small ghost, was our favorite butterfly. Folding its wings, it showed the face of an owl to its predators. Green-eyed wasps were almost as large as butterflies and it was important to notice the difference.

The jungle forest was beautiful. The canopy was so high we could hardly recognize the birds flying through it. Underneath were all the other species of plants struggling to utilize whatever sunshine filtered down—trees, shrubs, vines, and the bright flowers of epiphytes. Fungi erupted on rotting logs, some as lovely as creamy flower petals, others in astonishing shades of yellow, rust, or even blue.

One day on our return from the lake I started to step over a big stick when I realized the stick was a snake. My flying leap extended into several flying leaps before I turned around to see if the creature was following me. My husband did not dare to cross the snake because if it should suddenly move, he had nowhere to run. The scaly gray reptile held its head up, eyes rolling, while my husband photographed it. Then he bypassed the trail by cutting a detour through the forest.

Hiking to the lagoon was another story. It was a short trail but fraught with danger. Immediately we encountered a washout over which various and sundry aids (mostly logs of many shapes and sizes) weren't really much aid; but when we did manage to wade, balance, teeter, and slide, we entered the path only to find more of the same. So we lurched from log ramp to log ramp, often to find the ramp floating. When we reached a dry spot, we would stop to listen for birds. Heretofore, merely making progress had taken all our attention.

A canoe was kept at the lagoon. Late afternoon was the best time to float around the perimeter, hoping for the sight of a sungrebe, as well as a good time to walk a short distance on the main trail when the musician wren and the nightingale wren sang their haunting melodies. The nightingale wren's song is so beautiful that one late afternoon I played the tape of its call, and as I stood quietly the tiny brown bird (so small that at first I thought it was a butterfly) flew out and perched at my feet.

I cannot omit Sunset Point, a corner of land jutting out at the intersection of the Tambopata and the Rio del Torre. I wish I could paint a picture of the idyllic scene: grass encircled by bamboo, a bench where we often sat waiting for the evening flight of oropendolas, caciques, and macaws, and waiting for the orange-red sun to sink behind the forest on the other side of the river.

Sleep came early at the Explorer's Inn in spite of the rustling noises of the bamboo rats and the one-note song of the cinereous tinamou. But in the dim candlelight while the first birds called in morning darkness, we hurried out to answer the tremulous call of the tropical screech owl. Another day in the jungle had begun.

ESCAPE FROM THE AMAZON

February 1984

It was the best fried-egg sandwich I had ever eaten. The crispy brown edges dripped from the deep fat in the black iron frying pan. I was standing under the sweltering mid-morning Peruvian sun at Puerto Maldonado, listening to the *tap-tap* of the telegraph operator's machine behind the window of the little office of the two-room wooden shack called the "airport."

My husband and I had been wakened at three in the morning in our thatched-roof cabin at Explorer's Inn, a complex of a few small bamboo buildings on the Tambopato River, a tributary of the mighty Amazon. We had eaten our last breakfast of fresh-baked bread and hot coffee and carefully made our way along the uneven bamboo-slat pathway to the riverbank. In the dark we crept slowly down the slippery wooden steps, squashed over the muddy shore, and finally teetered across a wobbly gangplank and dropped into the big canoe.

A wooden roof covered the canoe, but rain beat in from the open sides, so I opened my umbrella, pointed it into the wind, and pressed it close to my body. Dawn came, but with scarcely a change in the hue of the sky. Our boatman sat unprotected on the stern and kept an eye out for floating debris ahead. Huts and small clearings emerged from the mist, and eventually the canoe was jammed onto the mud bank at Puerto Maldonado and we jumped to shore from the bow. Only seven-thirty, and the plane wasn't due until nine.

We were driven in an ancient Land Rover to the small airfield on a very lumpy and bumpy road, around washouts, in and out of holes, and over rocks. The airport was a drab two-room building where, on one wall, a snack bar advertised fried-egg sandwiches and Inca Cola.

Thomas, travel agent for the Explorer's Inn, was a rangy man, skin darkened by years of living under the African sun. He lived in Puerto Maldonado, a sprawling village of several dozen houses situated on the banks of the Tambopata, and he arranged for visitors to travel up and down the river. This morning, after his friendly greeting and helping hand as we debarked onto the muddy shore, he was frowning and shaking his head. He informed us there was a great probability that the airplane to Cuzco would not arrive because the clouds were so low on that high elevation that the airplane would not even take off from Lima. And only on the Cuzco run did the plane pick up passengers at this out-of-the-way river station. The telegraph operator at last stood up and shook his head. Bad news.

We were disappointed but not surprised when the flight was officially canceled. We considered alternatives. A drive back through the mountains would be a three-day trip, if we could find a vehicle and a driver. But luck was with us as our friend Carlos came running with good news: The Peruvian army plane that flew to Cuzco once every two weeks would soon leave and take as many passengers as could be piled on top of the cargo, and he had purchased tickets for us. "Half an hour," he said, and waved good-bye.

The rain abated, and I walked down the road, binoculars ready for any birdlife in the trees. That amused me for a while. We watched the *Hercules*, an old World War II cargo plane, still camouflaged with dark green and gray splotches, descend from the sky and roll onto the packed-dirt runway. Nearby stood two young businessmen in dark slacks and short-sleeved white shirts also waiting for a ride. Our spirits dimmed when the pilot decided to take only the passengers going to Iberia, a jungle village on the border of Brazil a short distance away. A flock of travelers of all ages and colors, loaded with every kind of baggage, piled into the gaping maw of the giant transport, which took off. It returned in an hour. Our turn.

Again our hopes of reaching Cuzco were dashed as we learned that the big plane had to first transport three tons of rice to Iberia. The hundred-pound bags were loaded one by one, carried on the backs of natives who appeared out of nowhere as word about the money-paying job reached the village. The chatter of propellers slowly turning, then the smooth singing of the flying blades, and our little group watched the transport take off.

Surprisingly, within an hour the camouflaged plane returned. But Thomas informed us that first *another* load of rice had to be delivered. This labor is one of the few chances a native Peruvian has to earn wages, but the process was a slow one.

As the plane began to move, it suddenly swung around and stopped. A flat tire! Another delay, but now we had a distraction. Something to watch. How does one jack up an airplane without mechanical assistance? Tired as I was, I was fascinated by the process.

First, several men carried a long wooden plank, which they

placed on the ground. Then the pilot ran the plane onto it, allowing several other strong men to wrench the wheel off. It seemed to take forever to repair the tire and remount it. By now it was so late that the pilot decided to take us, his passengers, with him to Iberia.

The only crew member, a very young uniformed army noncom, helped me climb into the cavernous body of the plane, where I found a quite comfortable spot somewhere on the mountain of bags of rice. We roared into the sky, but there were no windows out of which to catch a last glimpse of river or mountain. Within fifteen minutes we landed.

The rice bags were unloaded one by one by waiting villagers. We were ordered to deplane. On the grass runway around us, huge balls of raw rubber waited to be loaded. The children had been playing on them, rolling them around while trying to balance on top. Each enormous ball was pushed by men, women, and children and rolled up a ramp into the storage space of the aircraft. At last it was our turn to climb a ladder clamped to the rear doorway.

When we reboarded, the crewman took my arm and led me over the humps of rubber to a net basket hanging from the wall. Though I tried to object, as the only white woman I was destined to occupy the only proper seat, and I was too tired to argue. I idly wondered about all the times I had been instructed that, in the case of a drop in air pressure, a little yellow oxygen mask would drop in front of me. I drowsed. Presently I was aware of a soldier dressed in a green jumpsuit gently tapping my shoulder, placing a slender rubber tube into my hand, and guiding it to my mouth. I couldn't feel anything, but I knew I was taking in oxygen. So we flew over the Andes.

At five o'clock in the evening we climbed over the cargo of rubber balls and stumbled onto the tailgate of the plane to debark at the Cuzco airport, noting with mild interest that it was guarded by armed soldiers. It was with a sigh of relief that we made our way through the exit gate and decided we had a good chance of reaching Lima in time, maybe even with a day to spare.

Well, dear reader, does this seem to have been a long story? It had been a *long* day, and as we trudged away from the friendly giant, I smiled to myself. We hadn't even worn seat belts!

PART VI

AROUND THE WORLD

TANZANIA
February–March 1982

Before my husband and I departed on a monthlong birding safari in Tanzania, we watched countless TV wildlife programs and read many books about southern Africa.

They pictured native villages of round, grass-roofed huts, set in a circle so evil spirits could not find a corner in which to lurk. Or houses constructed by weaving saplings together and packing the open spaces with mud.

From *National Geographic* articles, we knew that native women dress in colorful wraparound garments, flowing robes cover their head and shoulders, and they bear huge baskets loaded with produce on their heads. As everyday garb, the warlike Masai tribesmen would be wearing stiff bead necklaces and flashing metal earrings hung from large pierced ears, and they would attempt to destroy anyone who tried to photograph them, because they believe the picture steals their spirit away.

We would be able to stop at outdoor bazaars where a tourist could trade his or her shirt and tennis shoes for an armload of carved figures and animals.

I sat entranced one evening for a full hour's TV documentary about termite mounds, and expected to find the landscape dotted with the three- to four-foot-high mud monuments now abandoned by their minute builders but inhabited by dwarf mongooses. The program led me to believe that in the Serengeti we would drive through hundreds of thousands of wildebeests and gazelles and herds of zebras, giraffes, and waterbuck, and if we were lucky we could watch cheetahs or a leopard stalk prey over the grassy savannah. Or we might be fortunate enough to observe the rare oryx of the stately tall horns, or glimpse a klipspringer momentarily silhouetted on a rock against the evening skyline, or the tiny, wide-eyed dik-dik hiding beneath a roadside bush.

George Schaller's *Golden Shadows, Flying Hooves* records his years of lion research at Seronera, so we were prepared to see lions devouring freshly killed zebra practically along Tanzania's only narrow bumpy road connecting Mt. Kilimanjaro with Lake Victoria. Or prides of lions sleeping daylight hours away under shading acacia trees.

Iain Douglas-Hamilton's *Among the Elephants* describes his tracking of the matriarchal elephant family groups, each individual named and becoming a personality. Those bad Tyrone sisters! Certainly we would come close enough to elephants to count the lines crisscrossing those rough, tough hides and see how the herd moved to protect the newly born babies.

We would find hippopotamuses submerged in pools, their pink ears and dull eyes protruding balefully, their cumbersome bodies shifting and snorting about.

We might overnight in a tent camp where lions roar at night, tramping elephants or cape buffalo wander dangerously close, and black kites scream at dawn. Or from the patio of a government-operated game lodge we might view a panorama of wildlife stretching as far as the eye could see; for example, giraffes stretching their long necks to bite off the thorny tops of trees, or tusked warthogs running pell-mell with tails erect like flagsticks.

And the birdlife would be fantastic. One would think saddle-billed storks would stand on the edge of ponds, with red-and-yellow-decorated bills coyly pointed downward, waiting to be photographed. Numerous fluffy-tailed ostriches should be common, either strutting by on ungainly, knobby-kneed legs or racing as if they were warming up for the Kentucky Derby. Barbets, firefinches, whydahs, bishops, and weavers would surround us with reds and yellows, and the iridescent green, violet, and scarlet sunbirds would dart like butterflies in and out of gold, flame, and pink flowering trees. Yellow or red-throated francolins, long-necked bustards, and crowned plovers would be up and about on cool early-morning drives. Large green-headed, red-winged turacos would try to hide from us in dark upper branches of highland forests.

And one should not forget about the possibility of hundreds of olive baboons scampering in the open woods, often with baby baboons catching a ride on the mother's back. Also blue monkeys, small Tarzans, swinging from tree to tree, causing an awful ruckus.

Do you believe this is Africa today? It is all true. I saw it with my own eyes!

TWO TALES FROM MAURITIUS ISLAND

September 1988

The Pink Pigeon

The search for the rare pink pigeon was one of the most unusual experiences of my life. There are probably only a dozen left in the wild. The pigeon breeds in the Cryptomeria forest, a rain forest on the island of Mauritius in the Indian Ocean. The trees are tall dark evergreens resembling the ponderosa pines of our West. And they are tall!

The trail leading to the forest first goes down a steep decline. It is narrow and wet and, in fact, is called "the hole." Only seven of us were able to reach the bottom of the trail, including Steve, a six-foot skinny young Brit doing research on the endangered Mauritius parakeet, and Frank, our guide.

The researchers had erected platforms in the tops of two of the tallest trees. A ladder to begin the climb extended only fifteen feet up the trunk. Steve was first up, and I followed. When there was no more ladder, I had to climb the tree itself, holding on to the branch above and placing my feet on the next slippery wet branch, thus slowly working my way to the top.

The last toehold was a very short limp branch; then Steve and I locked wrists and he helped me poke myself up through a hole cut into the platform. We were on a tiny square floor built of boards, a flimsy structure with no protective edges or railings. I was on top of the world, looking down on a huge valley and two mountainsides.

Two other birders came after me; there was barely room for the four of us, and nothing around but space. We remained there, sitting shoulder to shoulder, for two hours in the morning, gusts of rain periodically coursing down on us. Whenever the air cleared, we swept the far-off treetops with our binoculars for the sight of a flying pink bird. We did not see a pink pigeon. Well, we know one world-class birder, Joel Abrahamson, who made four trips to Mauritius before he located a pink pigeon, which actually flew down over the parking lot where they were standing by their vehicles! And we have heard other stories about birders who made return trips for that very reason.

On the return trip to the ground, the drop to the first branch was the scariest. As I looked down into the rain forest, I felt like one of the lemurs of Madagascar that perched in tall trees and looked down on us. Carefully, from branch to branch, I made my way down to the ladder and the safety of the trail, and began the climb out of "the hole."

I have been lucky in finding rare bird species, so I was disappointed, of course, not to catch a glimpse of the pigeon after so much effort. But the important thing is that the forest is being preserved to protect its habitat. So hopefully there will be pink pigeons forever.

Round Island

On Mauritius Island we met Wendy, a young woman who had been the director of the island's World Wildlife Fund research station for eight years and is wonderfully knowledgeable about the many endangered plants—endangered because of encroachment by humans who are cutting down the forests to plant sugarcane fields. As she was planning a field trip to Round Island to check on some rare plants and the two remaining palm trees, the only survivors of a species, she invited our birding group to go with her. She actually put us to work.

Round Island is rarely visited because of the difficulty of landing, and because there is no fresh water on it. The island is formed of basaltic rock that has been carved into strange swirling shapes etched by wind and blowing sand. In six trips to Mauritius, Frank had never been able to land on Round Island. The shore is composed of slippery rock, and the waves can be huge. This time we were on a fishing boat that could anchor offshore, and we carried a Zodiac inflatable boat for ferrying us to the island. First the crew went in and tied a strong rope to a rock on the shore. When we arrived, the crew pulled the Zodiac up close to the rock and held it while we clambered out.

Here we were close to the nesting seabird colonies. Flying around were white- and red-tailed tropicbirds, wedge-tailed shearwaters, and herald petrels; if we had tried to get good views of them with binoculars from a moving boat and at the same time steady ourselves on deck, we'd have been disappointed.

Once safely onshore, we slowly climbed to the top, encountering rather difficult footing at times because of the strange contour of the round rocks we had to slide ourselves over or circumvent. It was exciting to be with Wendy and Steve, young people concerned with the quality of our environment, who were documenting the slow extermination of plants and animals that live in such a delicate balance with nature and trying to save them and make the world aware that as we push the endangered species to the brink we are forever losing the links with our past—the lemurs, beautiful birds, trees, and flowers. Mauritius is the land of the extinct dodo, a flightless aberrant pigeon. In the small museum, which we visited later, one dodo skeleton remains from the many dodos reported by early explorers.

The island is so bare we could not even find a sheltered spot to eat our picnic lunches, which included big handheld wedges of pared pineapple. Wendy located several minute specimens of the rare plant she hoped to preserve. By noon we were sweltering in the tropical sunshine.

Then came the best part of our adventurous day. After descending precariously to the ocean shore, Frank and Wendy, whose attire included bathing suits, dived into the cool blue Indian Ocean. The decision was easy. In a flash I slipped off my jeans and tennies and dived in after them, leaving clothing and binoculars on the dock to be ferried back to the ship.

We swam underwater and looked at all the strange fish and reefs while the Zodiac made ferry trips out to the fishing boat. Surrounded by the vast Indian Ocean, I felt as free as the birds above and the fish swirling below me.

There was no way we could get back onto the rocky shore again, so we swam a long way through the gentle waves back out to the fishing boat, where I wriggled over the edge of the Zodiac and the laughing crew lifted me back on board. I pulled the top of a warmup suit over my head and hung my shirt in the wind to dry, which in the sunshine was almost immediately. And we were offered more wedges of the delicious sun-ripened pineapple.

Now I have swum in the hot springs of the ice caves of Iceland and in the cool water that flows uninterrupted to the edge of Antarctica—the top and bottom of the world!

THE SOUTH ATLANTIC: ABOARD THE *PROFESSOR KHROMOV*

March 1995

Our arrival in Ushuaia, Argentina, was weird, as the little plane from Buenos Aires put us down on a landing strip in a little country town, and from there we traveled by bus through the night and arrived at the Albatross Hotel at three o'clock in the morning.

It was afternoon before we walked down to the dock to view our ship, the *Professor Khromov,* a remodeled former Russian underwater research vessel, which had just arrived. We were met by a young Brit, Amanda, on her way home from a summer's Antarctic campout, where she had studied the effects, if any, on the pressure of tourism on the penguin colonies. There were ten passengers in all: three couples, two single ladies, and us, the only Americans.

We had a stateroom that was pretty roomy for a ship's cabin. Besides double-decker bunks we had a couch, a desk, a covered chair, a bath with a shower, and loads of storage space along the wall and under the bunks. Getting into the upper bunk required pushing a chair against the bunks and using the chair's back as a ladder. It was my bed for the duration.

Immediately we had boat drill, then left the dock at six. Already we were seeing familiar ocean birds: black-browed albatross and northern fulmar. We met our charming Russian captain, Philip, and our tour leader, Britain's Tony Roper.

Before dawn we were out in the open ocean. My alarm clock woke me at six. I dressed warmly, went down for coffee, which is always available, and then up to the deck before breakfast. Lots of black-browed albatross, giant petrels, and white-chinned petrels were soaring in the distance. I spent most of the morning on deck, where I saw flocks of Wilson's storm-petrels and our first wandering albatross. A *life bird*! Then another life bird, a thin-billed prion.

Late in the afternoon I asked someone on the staff if the sauna could be heated. It could. The sauna and hot shower felt great.

Tony explained that we would have "recap" every evening in the bar before dinner. So we started a bar chit and had a glass of wine.

From the deck early the next morning, lots of blue-eyed cormorants and a few South American terns were out and about. After breakfast the crew instructed us on safety rules during transportation in the Zodiacs, the bright orange rubber boats used for going ashore. I've found a sheltered spot on the bridge level where I am protected from the wind and can watch the sea in comfort.

After lunch we departed by Zodiac for our first landing in the Falkland Islands, New Island, and were joined by Ian Strange, author of *Field Guide to the Wildlife of the Falkland Islands and South Georgia*. We walked against the wind to a rockhopper penguin colony, though most of the birds had departed. There were fuzzy young of black-browed albatross and imperial shags.

After quite a long rocky climb, my husband found a good spot to rest and I took his camera down to the rookery and hoped to get some interesting photos. Walking back slowly through tussock grass and bare hills to the bay, we found striated caracaras, tussockbirds, Falkland Island steamer ducks, Falkland thrushes, siskins, swallows, rock cormorants, dark-faced ground tyrants, and pied oystercatchers. Then we took tea; bought stamps, a first day cover, and postcards; and caught the Zodiac back to the ship.

The evening movie was the first half of *Flight of the Condor*. We often watched a movie or documentary in the evening, including several David Attenborough documentaries. We really enjoyed the informative movies we saw on the unusual aspects of the continents.

I was always up at six and on deck for coffee and seabirds. The third morning we went ashore at Westport at seven-thirty. This is a typical treeless island where we were driven across the fields to see colonies of nesting birds. Black-browed albatross and rockhopper penguins inhabited every shelf in the cliffs. We took tea at an island farmhome. While we were there, a bush plane landed on the little landing strip, bringing a home teacher who would stay with the family's eleven-year-old daughter Holly for two weeks. Then she would visit other families and return in six weeks. I combed the beach for strange keyhole shells and stayed until the last Zodiac took me back to the ship at noon.

At two o'clock in the afternoon we were off for Carcass Island. We had a cross-country hike and climb through tough, weedy, tussock grass to gentoo and Magellanic penguin colonies. Then we still had a grueling two more miles along the edge of the coast with a strong wind blowing, and a climb straight up to a meadow with a sheep trail, up and down through gorse and high grasses, but finally we arrived at a farmhouse for tea. In a dining room furnished with dark, polished furniture, we found a beautifully laid table with twenty different kinds of little cakes and cookies. Apparently the local women look forward to the arrival of the tour ships. To save hiking all the way back to the shore, we packed into a Jeep, where I had to sit jammed against the gearshift in the front seat, and were driven over uncharted hilly fields. Finally we had only a short walk back to the beach and the waiting Zodiacs. Back on board the ship, I headed for the sauna. It felt wonderful! Besides penguins we had seen meadowlarks, black-crowned night herons, austral thrushes, and skuas.

We arrived at Port Stanley. The captain eased our ship up to the dock, and we debarked and boarded a bus for a tour of the island. We learned that the world's supply of squid, which is located by spotter planes, is harvested here. It rarely freezes in the Falklands, so vegetables are gleaned all winter long. For any serious health problems, individuals return to Britain and are covered by national health insurance. A British Antarctic survey plane, a Dash 7, a turbo-prop manufactured in Canada and also used by Norway and Greenland, was on the ground. FIGAS, the Falkland Islands Government Air Service, connects the many islands and is the air link to Punta Arenas, Chile, where once a week it connects with international flights. Otherwise, Falkland Islanders use the Royal Air Force TriStar to England, refueling at Ascension Island. At the dock we saw an Antarctica research vessel that had just returned from its summer season, loaded with scientific equipment of all kinds. We also saw rusted, sunken ships in the harbor, a reminder that recently a war had been fought here. NO WHALING signs were all over the place.

We had three days at sea before reaching the island of South

Georgia. As usual, I spent the mornings on deck. Soft-plumaged petrels are the most common seabirds and can be identified by their light, high, butterflylike flight. Sometimes I went up to the warm bridge and talked to the friendly officers, and I could study the charts and find our latitude. No one else used the sauna, which is unbelievable because its hot steam was so wonderful after a cold, windy day on deck.

Once I woke during the night to the extreme rolling of the ship, but I finally fell asleep again until breakfast call. Lots of seabirds circled in the high wind. It rained, and dolphins surfed alongside the ship. It was definitely getting colder. I returned to the lounge for tea, and the Brits were talking about an upcoming rugby match and hoping for an instant replay via satellite or over World Service radio.

The next day, after spending the morning in a sheltered corner near the stern, in the afternoon I sat curled up in a comfortable chair in the library and began reading. It was too stormy to show films in the lounge after dinner.

The following morning we anchored at Gritviken, South Georgia. For most of the night we had been tossed around in our bunks, but finally the ship quieted in lea of the island. The harbor was beautiful, with glaciers and snow-covered peaks in the background. There were only a few buildings, to house a small military force, and a small whaling museum. The caretakers live on a small sailboat anchored in a sheltered inlet. We walked the beach, where one pugnacious fur seal almost got my husband, but a crewman warned it off. The famous explorer Ernest Shackleton is buried here; we paid the traditional homage and drank a rum toast at his grave. We spent the whole morning ashore, then returned to the ship at noon to write postcards, as a government officer came on board with stamps for sale. All the island inhabitants came aboard for lunch. During the afternoon we traveled in Zodiacs to Nord-Glacier, where we found king, gentoo, and chinstrap penguins.

I arrived for my much-anticipated evening sauna and, to my surprise, encountered a nude man energetically swatting himself with green tree branches! The laundry lady quickly brought him a pair of trunks, and I joined him, but I rejected his offer of the branch ceremony.

We departed early for a harbor ride to view thousands of young hair seals and gentoo penguins. Our second Zodiac stop was at Prion Island, where some of our group hiked to the top to view wandering albatross nests. Our Russian crew seemed to love the shore trips, and one carried a sophisticated camcorder. The guys were helpful if the seals become obstreperous. I was wearing a wool turtleneck, a ragg wool sweater, a down vest, and a mountain parka! Here we found a new bird, a South Georgia pipit.

When we went ashore, we encountered thousands of king penguins, which were trusting and allowed us to walk among them, and certainly are not an endangered species. On the way back I stopped to watch a leopard seal trying to catch a penguin. The interaction looked like a game of tag. The sauna was out of order that evening, and I missed it.

Our next stop was Larson Bay, with a Zodiac trip up Grydvilken Fjord, where we watched giant petrels feeding on fresh seal, and the photographers had a field day. After lunch we anchored at Cooper Bay, where I finally saw macaroni penguins on shore rocks. They are numerous on South Georgia, but they breed on high, rocky slopes in protected bays that are difficult to sail into. The sea was quite violent, and we all rather tumbled into the Zodiacs. On climbing back onto the ship, we had to make a massive jump to reach the ship's ladder. The deckhands were skilled at helping us.

As we lay anchored in Royal Bay during a storm, I watched an interesting sight: king penguins swimming around the ship, holding their heads and necks up high out of the water. We were reeling from the waves. The weather station forecast that the storm would continue for three more days. We were leaving South Georgia for Tristan da Cunha, an unbroken sea journey of four days.

I found the ship's library on our deck with a treasure trove of adventure books. I got a copy of Louis Halle's *The Sea and the Ice* to read again, my third time.

We didn't get much sleep as our ship plowed through the billowy sea. Finally toward morning I dropped off. My days became a time of reading and occasionally going out on deck to watch the sea, necessarily bundling up each time. I stopped by the bridge and Captain Philip explained to me a TV readout for position at sea—we were fifty two degrees south. Tristan is at thirty-eight degrees. He could find the distance by plotting a straight line or a curved global line; the latter is faster.

I found diary accounts written by the ship captains of many polar expeditions, describing survival against all odds. Cold, wet, starving, and sick, they clung to life sometimes for a year or more before being rescued. Polar adventurers must be a breed apart. Captain Philip stamped and autographed my South Georgia map showing our route traced in red ink, for which ceremony he invited me into his private quarters, a cheerful large corner cabin with a radio and TV. We had tea together.

I slept fairly well in spite of the lurching ship. It became necessary to hold on to handrails to walk about. Dishes slid down the tables at mealtime, but wet cotton tablecloths prevented breakage.

I finished *The Sea and the Ice,* but the library was inaccessible all day because of a broken lock, so I remained outdoors on deck a lot in spite of the weather. I loved to watch the wandering and black-browed albatross and soft-plumaged petrels reel in the high winds, soaring and then dipping down into the huge white-capped waves.

Our recap hour was becoming ridiculous—one night we bet on the ship's mileage over the next twenty-four hours. The crew could not repair the library's lock, so the door was now left open. I found several more true adventure stories, and I couldn't seem to get enough of them. These days on board had given me the opportunity to read books I never knew existed. I found the overstuffed library lounge chairs the most comfortable place in the world.

We were approaching the Tristan da Cunha area, and the furious sea was moderating. At last there were no whitecaps, and we experienced sunshine for a change. The white-chinned petrels up here in the more northern latitudes have really white faces.

Our approach to Tristan da Cunha was comparatively calm. At last a much-wanted new bird appeared and was well seen: a yellow-nosed albatross. We were beginning to see greater shearwaters in numbers, a species we'd formerly seen in the North Atlantic. In early evening land was sighted in the distance. There are three islands in the group: Tristan in the center, Inaccessible to the west, and Nightingale to the east.

We discussed the history of Tristan before going ashore. On the island is a very small settlement begun by sailors cast ashore from wrecks and a few whaling captains from Massachusetts, with much inbreeding. Family relationships have been recorded for generations.

The island of Tristan da Cunha is inaccessible most of the year, and we almost didn't make the landing. The Zodiac departure was dangerous, and on arriving at the island, we had to scale a three-foot-high dock, assisted by the helping hands of islanders from above, in order to disembark near the small village of Edinburgh.

There was nothing special to see on the island, and after the first half hour of looking around the general store and wandering among the few houses, most of our party decided to return to the ship. But the local officials did offer some choices. We could visit their potato patches, of which they were very proud, or climb a three-thousand-foot mountain.

I chose the mountain and got into a truck with several people from our sister ship, the *Professor Molchanov,* which was on its way back to England and, according to a prearranged plan, was visiting Tristan at the same time as the *Khromov.* This was to give the Russian crews time to spend with their friends.

We drove to the beginning of the trail at the bottom of an escarpment and started out by crossing a meadow, then ascended on a trail so narrow that I didn't dare take my eyes from the ledge beneath my feet. About halfway up the mountain most of the climbers stopped under an overhanging shelter to rest, then decided to go no farther. I had lunch in my day pack and thought I'd find a sheltered cove in the rocks and spend the rest of the day just sitting and enjoying the scenery.

The summit looked very far away. The few hikers forging ahead, wearing bright parkas, made colorful spots against the mountain. They eventually reached the tree line and disappeared, and that is when I made up my mind that I would try to reach the top too.

I shouldered my day pack, then continued up through grass and scattered rocks, zigzagging along the well-worn sheep trail. One of the two local guides assigned to accompany the climbers dropped back and walked with me; as the morning progressed, he offered to carry my pack, and I gratefully handed it over.

As we neared the summit, we came to hanging ropes, which we used to pull ourselves up the steep path. We also found some rubbery bushes whose branches we held on to. At last we arrived at steps dug into the hillside, and at that point I knew I would make it to the top. My guide and I emerged onto a brilliant, sunshiny glade, where our young Brits from the *Khromov,* Sean and Amanda, and two other British women were already resting.

Just in time for lunch! On all sides of us the blue ocean lay far below. Then, as I lay on my back looking at the sky, a pair of sooty albatross flew over in a synchronized mating dance, swirling and diving in unison! This was a bonus—a once-in-a-lifetime, unexpected, miraculous spectacle.

At first the trip down wasn't too difficult because we had ropes to let us down the steep areas. But when we reached grass, I sat down and slid, as my leg muscles were already hurting. The guides laughed at that. Finally Amanda and I chose to shorten the descent by sort of skiing in long glides across an area of scree (sand and stones). As my legs turned to rubber, I would sit for a few minutes, then stumble down again until, finally at the bottom, we sank onto the ground and rested.

We had to cross the meadow and the dry rocky streambed again, and from there to the truck, which was waiting to carry us back to Edinburgh. There, at the general store, I bought a hand-dipped ice-cream cone. I bought an island patch at a little museum as a gift for my husband, who had been unable to make the day trip, then sat on a grassy hill, gazing out to sea in the late afternoon, waiting for the last Zodiac to come for us.

Reboarding the ship proved a dangerous process. Finally the crewmen lashed the Zodiac to the ship with heavy hawsers, but the waves dashed at the ship until the gangplank loosened, and over the widening sea below, we had to leap from the

Zodiac to the *Khromov*. At recap time, my mountain exploit was termed "brilliant" by Amanda and Sean, the only others from the *Khromov* to reach the top of the mountain.

Nightingale Island is a dream place for a birder to visit. It is a lonely rock island where landing is possible only under perfect conditions. We had to jump from the Zodiac onto rock piles covered by a seething surf. As far as anyone knows, our tour ship is the first to have landed birders there, and my husband and I were especially eager to land because our friend from South Africa, Dr. Peter Ryan, did a research project on speciation of the finches on both Nightingale Island and Inaccessible Island, and we had read his doctoral dissertation.

We had only two hours ashore, and I would have liked to stay all day. After pushing my way up through dense grass, I came out into a huge meadow with grasses growing as tall as I. I followed a narrow trail up toward the summit, finding many tristan buntings and thrushes. I had hoped to find the rarer Wilkins' bunting, and would have if we had had more time. Greater shearwater burrows were everywhere, and the parent birds dove aggressively at me. The young men of Tristan were on Nightingale for the annual digging of guano, which they would sell for the manufacturing of fertilizer on the mainland. They have great difficulty landing on Nightingale, so they camp out there for several weeks.

One of our British companions had a special mission there too, as a scientist friend had asked her to look for a newly recognized marine worm species on Nightingale. We all looked, but couldn't find the proper habitat. We returned the pilots to Tristan after circling Inaccessible Island with Peter's map in hand. This was a day to remember!

We celebrated the ship's birthday at a noon party in the bar with the captain and the mates. The *Professor Khromov* had been christened as a marine research vessel in Finland. In midafternoon we passed Gough Island, an impressive rock island rising out of the ocean with steep cliffs on all sides. South Africa maintains a weather station there, but no one is allowed to land. Gough Island has an endemic rail, but we sailed by wistfully, having contented ourselves with viewing the flocks of pelagic birds we now so easily recognized.

We would have a four-day run from Tristan to South Africa. The days were getting warmer and the seas smoother. I would watch the ocean from the upper deck in early afternoon and read the rest of the day.

The sea was becoming very calm, with birds resting on the shallow ocean swells all around the ship, mostly albatross and petrels. Sean and Amanda gave a slide presentation of their three months on Cuverville Island on the Antarctic Peninsula at the entrance to the Lamaire Channel.

There were flocks of Cory's shearwaters on the ocean, only a few albatross, and quite a few of the white-faced variety of white-chinned petrels. Our Russian crewman showed us a video of our Nightingale landing and other of our landings. He really did a good job with his camcorder.

The waves became huge, but I didn't have too much trouble walking about the ship. Sunshine flooded the deck, but there were only a few birds around. On our last day at sea the waves were moderate and we had a warm seventy-degree day. Everybody spent lots of time on deck. In festive moods, we all dressed for dinner.

We entered the harbor at Cape Town, South Africa, in calm waters, with everyone on deck. Customs officials came aboard, and we had quite a wait for permission to land. My husband and I didn't know what to expect on arriving at Cape Town because our reservation at an ocean resort had been unexpectedly canceled the day before our departure from home, though their agent had promised to provide us with a place to stay. A friendly agent from the Monkey Valley resort met us when we debarked.

Yeah, *Monkey Valley*! We stayed in a honey-colored log cabin with full housekeeping facilities, a loft with twin beds, a sofa, a table with four comfortable chairs, a bath with a shower, and a lovely veranda that looked out over the ocean. We dined at the resort's tiny restaurant with fine linen, candlelight, and wine. We drank a toast to the *Professor Khromov*, which had made possible one of the best adventures of our lives!

PART VII

PLEASANT INTERLUDES

OCTOBER IN DEATH VALLEY

October 1975

We parked our small travel trailer in Furnace Creek Campground, which has disorderly rows of campsites tucked under scattered mesquite trees, and everybody owns a picnic bench and charcoal grill. The sun beats down all day, but actually there is always a little breeze and one can be very comfortable in the shade. Death Valley National Monument is three thousand square miles of desert, most of which is salt upon which no life can grow, and temperatures can be extreme. Rugged mountains dominate gentle, fan-shaped slopes. Rain is almost nonexistent.

We played golf every other day at Furnace Creek Golf Course, and we could not help birding on the way around! We started at seven o'clock, first tee time of the day, and finished about ten-thirty, had a soft drink at the open air lunch stand, chatted for a few minutes, then took off to explore. The golf course was an oasis, with lush watered fairways, shrub borders, rows of towering date palms, scattered water hazards, and bunkers. Most mornings roadrunners dashed from under cover, then quickly dived back again, trailing long white-tipped tails. Flocks of blackbirds, starlings, grackles, and a lone brown-headed cowbird giddily flew off the freshly seeded greens to reassemble en masse nearby. Winter-plumaged sparrows (chippies, golden-crowned, fox, song, Lincoln's, lark, white-crowned, and Harris's) challenged our expertise. On the pond we noticed coots, eared grebes, a sora rail, a Canada goose, and a snow goose.

We were doomed to no "sleep-ins" on this vacation. Alternating with golf days, we were up before dawn when we drove to visit Death Valley's different habitats. A special destination was Mesquite Springs; we departed for the campground in the north in the dark at five-thirty, not meeting another vehicle on the road. We ate a picnic breakfast at dawn, then spent several hours looking for a LeConte's thrasher, which was supposed to be a resident bird. Mesquite Springs spreads out along a wide arroyo. The cracked clay floor of the blazing hot dry streambed fans out in fascinating designs of geometric figures: great oblongs, medium-sized squares, swirls of hexagons, and minute mosaics. Chameleons slip in and out of the cracks. Once there had been a huge lake here, formed by melting water flowing from Sierra Nevada glaciers during the last Ice Age. Forces of faulting, folding, vulcanism, erosion, and deposition created the landscape and continues to do so. A recess under a projecting ledge offered shade for our lunch stop. As we were about to leave the campground, we noticed that water trickled from a pipe near the gate, and around the water source grew some green trees. And that is where we found the LeConte's thrasher, in an unlikely habitat at an unlikely time of day!

One day we decided to drive through Titus Canyon. We had met a man who told us that he had driven his Pinto through and had seen a bighorn sheep. The drive through the canyon is only one-way for twenty-eight miles! No buses or trailers are allowed. No services. There are all kinds of printed warnings about the narrow dirt roads. We entered from the east a little after noon and reached the exit at four-thirty, mostly driving about five miles per hour.

But it was like being on another planet. One minute we would be hanging on a curve, looking up and barely seeing daylight. A few minutes later we'd be staring down into a funnel-shaped bowl. A roller-coaster ride at slow speed!

Colors changed from reds to blacks, browns, and greens. After we arrived at the highest pass, we had difficulty holding the van tight to the mountain as we turned and twisted down. A vehicle the size of an ant moved far below, but we caught up with it when the occupants stopped to watch a bighorn ram near the road. But two thoughtless women jumped out and chased it to get a better look, and it disappeared into a safer valley.

Just when we assumed that the end of the drive was near, a sign reading TITUS CANYON directed us into a six-mile continuously curving road that obviously had long ago been the winding river that carved out the canyon. It was twilight the whole way, though occasionally we could peer up and see a protruding peak bathed in sunshine. Our own frailty contrasted with the magnificent structures through which we passed. At last we emerged back into the late afternoon sunshine.

One of our first evenings we walked to the end of the little airport runway and beyond to a fenced sewage pond (wouldn't you know we'd find a sewage pond even out here!). It was growing dark, and across the pond six coyotes hungrily eyed a coot and a duck on the water.

Then we saw a bobcat on the golf course. It was hiding in

the bank of one of the ponds, hoping a coot would swim near enough to catch.

One day we took a picnic lunch and drove to Daylight Pass (about forty-five minutes into a mountain range) to search for a chukar partridge. While wandering over the area, I flushed a covey of chukar. It took another hour to locate them again, after we spent a good bit of time kicking around in shrubby clusters of thickets. It is amazing how so many fairly large birds can hide in so little space, and after they are flushed, disappear into thin air.

Dante's View is one of the highest and hottest places in Death Valley, and we were determined to climb the five miles from the parking lot at the main highway to the top. We started out so early that the planet Mercury was still visible on the horizon, but we had the advantage of the morning coolness and the lovely quiet from no sounds of traffic, at least during the first hours of our travel. Sage sparrow, stick pins decorating their white shirtfronts, sang tinkling songs to the rising sun. Buffy rock wrens bobbed around stone outcroppings. A wicked-eyed loggerhead shrike searched the desert for a bit of breakfast. Shimmering heat waves rose from the baked earth. A sign near a huge water barrel read DO NOT DRINK. FOR VEHICLES ONLY! We perched on the barrel, looked back on the mesquite-dotted desert below, and craned our necks upward to view the rocks on the ridge leaning crazily against one another. A few motorists offered us rides, but we had planned for this day for so long that we really wanted to arrive completely on foot. At last we reached the top, and gazed down on miles of waterless salt pan and acres of black salt hummocks. To the northeast, in the distance, sun shafts flickered on layered pink, mauve, and green strata of the Panamint Range. And we reveled in the sweep of the wild wind.

To escape the heat of the desert, we drove into the cool high mountains of Wilderness Canyon, a change from the desert valley floor to a pinyon-juniper montane forest. This is where the Shoshone Native Americans spent their summers. It is also where the early park rangers spent their summers, before the advent of air conditioning. Centuries-old bristle-cone pine still live on Telescope Peak. We parked our van at the picnic area and climbed most of the day, though we didn't reach the top. We found golden-crowned kinglets in the forest on the way back. The mountains are fresh and beautiful, but we wouldn't trade them for the more exciting life below.

We started at dawn one morning to make a trip to a birding "hot spot" that isn't on the map. We never leave home without stuffing our day packs with crackers, cheese, fruit, granola bars, trail mix, or any combination of those, plus Kool-Aid, cans of pop, and a jug of water. Even though we intend to return before noon, experience has warned us that we seldom do. We followed the directions of a park ranger to the end of Old Ghost Road, parked beside a doorless, windowless cabin, climbed up a completely dry gravel canyon to a hidden spring, and discovered a small green forest. Old Ghost Road is not listed under famous places in the park. It is not much more than a seldom used track that trails away from the staff living quarters and peters out near the abandoned cabin. At the hidden spring a long-billed marsh wren scolded, Say's phoebes sallied forth and returned to their perches. An alert kestrel peered down from his observation post on a defunct telephone pole. Down, down, down into the wooded canyon we worked our way, and we found a timid lost hermit thrush, a species classified on the park checklist as "unusual."

Noon is not the conventional time to stop at Salt Creek, a marsh with a boardwalk and not a tree in sight. Pupfish live in the little marsh pools. They are very rare small fish that over twenty thousand years ago adapted to living in water *six times* as salty as the ocean. In the winter when the water becomes cold, the little fish lie dormant in the bottom mud; when the water warms in the spring, the fish become active again. Some of them were isolated in different environments, so there are four different species of pupfish in Death Valley and five additional kinds outside its boundaries. The ones at Salt Creek are found nowhere else on earth. At noon the hot sun beat down unmercifully and the pupfish were not easy to find. Savannah sparrows fled from under the boardwalk into the marsh grass at the sound of our approaching footsteps. We finally found the little pupfish in a shallow pool at the very end of the trail. We watched them for a long time, in spite of the steamy weather, because we were also looking into the endless pool of the past.

We are not very good at sightseeing, but we stopped just long enough to take a photograph of a ghost town, Rhyolite. During the Gold Rush, gold and silver were found in enough quantity in this area to create boom towns. Rhyolite was the largest, with churches, an opera house, and twenty-five saloons; today there is only one building still standing—constructed completely out of glass beer bottles.

Driving these deserts and canyons at various times of the day reveals Death Valley in many lights and shadows. Miles of sand dunes appear golden coming from the west but dark brown in the late afternoon. One peak is named Corkscrew, but when it is photographed in both sun and shade it looks entirely different. Its layers of colored strata resemble mountains of agate. By five o'clock in the afternoon, it is too dark to see even one's footsteps, and the stars in the sky are already brilliant and the air suddenly becomes icy cold.

We saved our final walk for the sand dunes. Fourteen square

miles stretched to the horizon, flat and white at noon, shades of gold and brown like waves on a sea in late-day shadows. Barefooted, we dug our toes into the warmness, delighting in the simple act of stooping to examine a tiny mouse track in the sand. We turned to bid farewell to the blue hills, the essence of the vast desert. In a valley not more than ten miles wide between high mountains, we had witnessed astonishing geologic phenomena: salt flats, badlands, precipitous canyons, marshes, a creek, a forest, snowcapped mountain peaks, all shimmering silently in the heat under the endlessly deep blue sky.

Many people loved this land and learned to live here through its intemperate seasons. We learned to love it too.

THE DRY TORTUGAS: A TROPICAL PARADISE

1981–1987

The small floatplane softly splashes down off Garden Key, a coral island in the Gulf of Mexico. We slip out onto the struts; jump ashore; quickly unload our tents, our packs, and a foam cooler filled with ice; and hurry toward the few sheltering trees, where we will establish our camp for the next ten days. We are returning to paradise after a year's absence, remembering the dawn's coolness, the day's burning sun, the sand underfoot, and the glorious sunsets.

The few visitors to the island are tourists, fishermen, or vacationing sailboaters, who come ashore to picnic or browse around the ruins of Fort Jefferson, whereas we are there because it is part of one of the most fascinating centers of bird life in North America: the Dry Tortugas. A group of small keys without fresh water, they comprise the nesting grounds of thousands of sooty and noddy terns with visiting privileges for magnificent frigate birds and a surprising number of migratory birds that land to rest before flying north in early May to their summer breeding grounds.

Fort Jefferson, a monstrous ruin, was built with slave labor out of sixteen million bricks during the Civil War era and still exists as a national monument, where tourists come by seaplane for three-hour tours, inspect the crumbling ramparts, and return to Key West in time for lunch. One can run around the island in fifteen minutes. The fort became a federal prison, and it was here that Dr. Samuel Mudd was incarcerated after he was accused of caring for John Wilkes Booth following the assassination of President Lincoln, and here he became a hero for his discovery that the tropical disease malaria was carried by mosquitoes that bred in the stagnant pools.

A friend once asked me, "What on earth do you do all day on such a small island?" My quick reply was, "I watch birds. I am so busy that at lunchtime I grab crackers and peanut butter from the picnic table and rush out again."

Yet even I was surprised by my answer and struggled to recall the day-to-day activities that create such strong ties to this unusual habitat that we return to the mainland with reluctance at the end of our stay and return each year with such anticipation.

The continual bickering in the noisy seabird colonies on adjacent Bush Key is a daily predawn greeting, and as we emerge to the first light of day, frigate birds already float like black etchings on a pale pink canvas, motionless over the corner of the fort. We hasten past the locked portcullis inside the moat surrounding the shadowy, forbidding brick structure of the fort on our way to inspect remnant pilings from former coaling docks, a rusty black iron boundary and favorite perching site of noddy terns. In the tern world they are mavericks; instead of the typical white body wearing a black cap, the noddies are chocolate brown and sport white beanies. The handsome sooty terns, jet black above and white underneath, with deeply forked tail and call of "wide-a-wake," never cease the feeding run out to sea and back.

Each new day we point our telescope across the barracuda- and shark-infested channel and occasionally discover a stray brown- or red-footed booby perched on a dead branch on the opposite shore. The ungainly brown pelican amazes us with his agile dives for food. Delicate roseate terns reflect the morning sun on pale pink breasts.

Later each day, after the monument ranger opens the fort gates, we monitor the huge inside courtyard for new bird arrivals. We peer up into every tree, climb the spooky dark tower staircases to the grass-covered roof, check hiding places in weedy rubble heaps, and keep an eye on a brick water fountain, which, of course on this dry acreage, attracts all sorts of species.

Actually, the best place to see passerines is in our own campsite, where they are attracted to our offering of fresh water from an aluminum pie pan birdbath. From webbed camp chairs we relax and admire the warblers, thrushes, cuckoos, buntings, and other species that are fortunate enough to find our water supply. One day a parrot invaded our treetop above our lookout. That entertained us until the owner of a small sailing ship came to claim his pet.

Undoubtedly, the most famous bird of the Dry Tortugas is the white-tailed tropicbird. Always rare, some years not sighted at all, like a silver arrow it streaks toward our island, makes a low pass, and is gone. The observer forever retains the image of a white bird graceful as an angel, a swift beat of wings, and, at last, against the bright blue tropical sky, the display of long whipping tail feathers, longer than the bird itself. The almost mythical fairy-tale birds whip like blithe spirits across the sky, sometimes skim the waves, sometimes shoot up into the heavens. The sightings never cease to thrill us.

I remember one day I looked up while I was washing clothes in the sea and the beautiful silver silhouette hovered over me for several minutes. Another morning I witnessed an astonishing sight—a pair of tropicbirds speeding on a fixed course right down the channel! Whenever the bird comes into view, first as a familiar dot on the horizon, the shout "Tropicbird!" floats across our island. Once during our stay three ornithologists from the Smithsonian Institution camped beside us for three days, but no tropicbird appeared even though we all watched the sky from the four corners of the fort roof every morning. Not fair.

Small groups of birders arrive at this optimal time of year, the first ten days of May, remain only a few hours, view the nesting terns, and are gone again. For several years we made friends with members of the Sierra Club who camped nearby. Once when they departed, they left thirty gallons of water in plastic bottles on our picnic table!

The helicopter landing pad at South Point provides a marvelous outlook toward Loggerhead Key. (A white-winged dove and I rendezvous at the heliport every midmorning on my inspection round.)

Bright little orange, black, and white ruddy turnstones are regulars along the two sandy sides of our key. On the other two sides a brick wall encloses a moat, where one can lie on one's stomach and become engrossed in watching the tropical fish that dart among the shadows and the swaying underwater plants. The fish are yellow and black, red, silver with blue stripes, black with horns, new and different ones every visit. We became "fish listers" and purchased a small illustrated tropical fish guide.

Black-bellied plovers in varying degrees of spring moult commonly spend a couple of days on our beach, and once a golden plover stopped by. Uncommon arrivals were a white-rumped sandpiper, Canada goose, and lesser black-backed gull. Fiddler crabs frantically dig holes in the sand; they are amusing to watch during the hot part of the day when bird life is quiet.

We take turns manning the noddy watch throughout the day, hoping for a special prize—the black noddy.

After a two o'clock swim, the damp brick cells inside the fort and clusters of mushroom-shaped oaks provide shelter for the hot afternoon hours. Odd sightings are a dozen yellow-billed cuckoos at a time, a purple gallinule hunched on a narrow brick ledge, a sora rail sitting in the top of a tree, water thrushes and ovenbirds pecking around the low ground cover, a flash of merlin wings, a short-eared owl peering down, a black-crowned night heron. Even a white-throated sparrow was an island "first." In good years all the eastern warblers tumble down to rest, and they are everywhere, so we step carefully.

Some days we paddle our inflatable raft across the channel and down the length of the keys until we reach the open gulf. Out there we discover the light phase of the Louisiana heron. We are not allowed to walk on the other islands, but we wade in waist-deep water and photograph the tern chicks and fledglings. To my husband's dismay, I sometimes swim back across the channel.

I am the supplier of food after we have consumed the few fresh items we brought with us. I fish for mangrove snapper off the dock and I am good at it. We grill the fillets over a charcoal fire in the magic moments of sunset.

The sun dips behind us in early twilight, providing perfect light for a last telescope view toward Bush Key.

And *that* is why I am so busy on such a tiny island!

HEAVEN ON EARTH

November 1989

Where is it? It lies in the Tasman Sea between New Zealand and Australia, with nothing between it and the South Pole to break one's view over the ocean.

What is it? It is an island. Barely a dot on a map of the world, born from a volcanic eruption some seven million years ago, Lord Howe Island, six and a half miles long and one and a half miles wide, sits askew on the true north and south line from pole to pole. It merits a listing on the World Heritage Foundation for its rare collection of plants, birds, and marine life and for its exceptional natural beauty.

How about its history? Lord Howe Island was spared the ugly years of nearby Norfolk Island, where the worst criminals were sent from prisons in England during the colonization of Australia. Ecologically intact, in 1882 Lord Howe Island was declared the New South Wales Botanic Reserve. There are more birds and mammals on the island than residents.

Statistics, logistics, and history are hard concepts. We have something different here. Let's start over.

Lord Howe Island is fringed by soft coral, sand beaches, towering cloud-tipped mountains, and palm trees sighing by the shore, and it boasts a lagoon that sparkles blue in the sunshine. Halfway up Ned's Beach Road, about a half-mile from the shore, we found a rose-covered cottage for rent. This became our home for four wonderful days, as we had spontaneously left Australia for a short side trip.

Our first destination after asking for directions was Thompson's store, downhill from the cottage, for a supply of food. We would do our own catering. We bought bread, cereal, eggs, milk, oranges, and some canned items that would do nicely for our stay. The climb back up the hill was rather steep, but on arriving, we looked back down on a cove dotted with rocky outcroppings and islets. If I were an artist, I would paint this scene!

The first morning, as we began our exploration of the island, we heard the soft purring calls of the fairy terns, which nest in natural depressions of the Norfolk pines that border the shoreline road. Fairy terns must be the closest thing to angels. Their pure white wings, translucent against the sun, dazzled our eyes as the birds flitted among the trees that bordered our path.

We continued along the coast road to investigate the nine-hole golf course that had been constructed over a bushy and short grass area. We sat on a bench in the sunshine, expecting at any moment to see an endemic rail emerge from the marshy border; suddenly, there it was.

At dusk a local fisherman came, as he had promised when we met him on the beach earlier, and drove us in his truck to the edge of a wood in order for us to watch a phenomenon that occurs nightly during the shearwater breeding season. It was completely dark when hundreds of flesh-footed shearwaters flew in from their daytime foraging over the ocean, descended through the canopy, crashed onto the forest floor, and scuttled to their young in their nests. How did they know?! We covered our heads with our arms to protect ourselves from the onslaught. The show was magnificent.

We found walking trails through the subtropical rain forest in remote areas, and our favorite was the trail that led to the mountainous end of the island, where Mt. Lidgbird and Mt. Gower, at 2,870 feet, dominated the southern coast. While we enjoyed our picnic lunch, we could watch flocks of gray ternlets, small seabirds, that flew low over the water searching for schools of small fish or crustaceans near the surface; they never ceased their quick skimming and hovering. And at the end of the climb to the mountaintop, a vista lay before us, where many dark, rocky islands stretched out into the blue ocean, completely different from the soft sand beaches and coral reefs on this side of our island.

Our second night, at dinnertime, the fisherman stopped by with a gift of freshly caught and cleaned tuna, but he wouldn't stay to dine with us. We were disappointed because we knew he could tell us stories. The following day he took us in a small boat out around the headland and among the small islands, where the ternlets dipped their wings so close we could almost touch them. We dipped our fingers in the cool sea and marveled at the beauty surrounding us.

Every evening after dinner we would walk down Lagoon Road, the road leading to Windy Point and the little airstrip, at the same time scanning the cliffs on our left for the favorite perch of a huge owl, or so we had heard. We never did see it, but the exciting possibility was much more fun than going to a movie or out dancing. Besides, after our daytime adventures we were tired and ready to sleep peacefully in our rose-covered cottage.

As is often the case in close-knit communities, the emporiums took on the names of their owners. So we had Trader Nick's, Joy's Store, Leanda Lei, and Larrup's Boutique. And we soon learned the landmarks that either shortened our route or enticed us to find them: Ned's Beach, Signal Point, Kim's Lookout, Blinky Point, and Lover's Bay.

The island's first trolley system began the day we arrived. A little white bus crisscrossed the island about once every hour or so, and since there was no schedule, if we wanted a lift, we would wait at the corner of Anderson Road and Mutton Bird Drive or farther down at Skyline and McGee. And if we encountered the bus and driver along our way, we would just wave.

Our last night on Lord Howe Island, we made a deal with the bus driver. He picked us up and drove us to a lovely restaurant, the Lorhiti. There we celebrated our good fortune at finding this out-of-the-way place, the most fantastic unplanned interlude of our lives and a magical holiday.

We are happy that the World Heritage Foundation is keeping an eye on heavenly Lord Howe Island.

PART VIII

NICE PEOPLE

THE LAUNDROMAT LADY

July 1973

My husband and I had been camping on Kodiak Island, Alaska, for a few days of birding and fishing following a week's sojourn on St. Lawrence Island, an Inuit island in the Bering Sea and a ferry boat ride down the peninsula from the town of Seward, so one day I bundled almost all our clothing into two pillowcases and carried them off to the Kodiak Laundromat. Another woman entered a few minutes later, lugging five baskets of heavy-duty jeans, shirts, jackets, and socks. As she busily sorted items and filled all the other machines, she informed me that she and her husband worked a fishing boat all summer and came ashore only once for supplies and to wash clothes. She would be back on board, and off for another two months, by afternoon.

As I watched the colors tumbling and circling in the dryers, I casually asked the lady who managed the Laundromat where we might buy some king crab, a treat we had anticipated ever since our camping summer in Alaska was in the first planning stages. "This is not the time of year for king crab," she answered.

"But my husband brought home three Dungeness crabs yesterday. We think they are the best. Let me give them to you." I stammered in embarrassment and tried to make it clear that I really wanted to pay for them. Nothing would do but that I write down her address and promise to stop by after three o'clock in the afternoon to pick up the crabmeat.

It was raining as we drove off to explore the island and look for birds from the security of our vehicle. Black oystercatchers probed the stony beach with their bright red bills. Tufted puffins buzzed offshore like fat insects. Through the mist a pine grosbeak silhouetted himself on the top branch of a small pine tree.

By the time we arrived back in Kodiak it was after five o'clock, but I remembered my promise to the Laundromat lady, and somehow I knew she'd be disappointed if we did not accept her generous offer of fresh Alaska crab. She answered my knock as if she had been waiting for us, and from her kitchen she brought out and handed to me not only three big Dungeness crabs but a plastic bag full of several pounds of frozen king crab.

"We're moving," she explained as she pressed the heavy package into my hands, while I protested that her offering was too much. "I am so happy that I can give the crab to you. Something special for you to remember about Alaska."

She could not have chosen a more appropriate day to donate her supply of seafood. I had promised to contribute the meat for a dinner club of nine people. We had become acquainted with a young Kodiak schoolteacher named Judy, who at the moment was entertaining her sister and several friends who were vacationing from Judy's hometown in Minnesota, and a few neighbors had joined our nightly group. Each evening I brought our day's salmon catch to her trailer home, and she and her friends supplied heaps of tossed salad and French bread.

We boiled the crab in Judy's biggest kettle. We piled the white chunks onto our plates, then went back for more. We could not consume all of the gigantic supply!

The social hour that followed supper, with our animated chatter as we shared our varied experiences of the day, warmth and laughter against the rain outside, further endeared us to this wild but friendly land. We realized that, in accepting the gift offered with such generosity, we had given pleasure to the giver. We couldn't repay her, but someday in the future we would remember to pass on a gift of our own.

We added the Laundromat lady to our list of Nice People.

THE REXALL LADY

May 1975

My husband and I stopped in Yucca Valley, California, for a one-item shopping spree because our tube of toothpaste had disappeared at our last campground. Rose Canyon Road, a relic of old mining days, had challenged our driving skills all morning but had provided excellent birding. During our morning coffee break as we perched on the red rocks of a winding streambed, our very first rock wren put on a good show. Now I dashed into the corner Rexall store while my husband went off to refuel our station wagon.

To my dismay, as I carried my lone purchase toward the cashier's counter, a long line of parcel-laden customers blocked my progress. Teetering stacks of paper products, cleaning aids, toys, and every imaginable thing overbalanced the weary waiting shoppers. My luck to hit the big day in Yucca Valley—the annual Rexall one-cent sale!

I dangled my single item, very obviously inviting permission to move up in line. No go. Conversations and comments engulfed my continuous shifting from one foot to the other. Fortunately, the lady behind me drew me out of my reverie: She asked about the binoculars hanging around my neck.

Now *that* was a more interesting subject than other people's babies! Eagerly I described my morning adventure in the canyon and carried on enthusiastically about the hobby of birding until she probably was sorry she had asked. But when I mentioned that we were on the lookout for a Bendire's thrasher, she startled me with her reaction. "We have one in our rock garden every day," she told us. She described the rock garden and followed up this intriguing information with a command: "You must go up there. I won't be home for another hour or two, but there are chairs in the shade of the patio overhang. You take highway . . . turn left on . . . street, third house on the right. Our name is on the mailbox."

Eventually my turn arrived to pay, and I raced out to my concerned husband, who sat in the driver's seat perspiring profusely in the noon sun and wondering if his wife had been kidnapped or had suffered heat stroke.

We leisurely consumed our picnic lunch and iced tea while sitting on the Rexall lady's patio. Rocks of all colors, spaced in pleasing patterns, surrounded a spraying water fountain. A hare with the longest ears I've ever seen on a rabbit hopped within its borders. Then the thrasher ventured out from a sage thicket. We didn't know whether to laugh or to cry; the thrasher was not our target bird. It was a very healthy specimen of a California thrasher. But the whole adventure had been such fun, and birders don't always win.

A car entered the driveway and two people got out. The Rexall lady's husband appeared quite startled to see strangers at home on his patio. We laughed and introduced ourselves all around. Our hosts were a doctor and his wife who lived in San Francisco but who flew to their desert hideaway on weekends. These Nice People conducted us on a tour of their spacious abode, served us cold lemonade, and waved a friendly farewell as we returned to wild thrasher country.

MR. TOM

May 1977

The Bachman's warbler is probably extinct. The bright yellow flittery four-incher resembles a hooded warbler, but reports of sightings are rare and lately not well confirmed. I know expert birders who, after consulting the earlier literature, have searched in the proper habitat, mostly the I'on Swamp of South Carolina, for as long as three weeks during the breeding season and neither seen nor heard a Bachman's.

Like diving for sunken gold or digging for buried treasure, searching for a rare bird carries a high degree of excitement. Once in Michigan's Upper Peninsula I spent an afternoon patiently working my way through filings in an old gold mine in the hope of discovering an overlooked chunk of the pure shining metal. A day later I repeated the monotonous procedure and proudly extracted a small irregular piece of pure copper. The end result was not as important as the intense expectancy of the hunt.

My husband and I were on the final leg of a May birding holiday, heading north from Key West to a Memorial Day pelagic trip off Ocean City, Maryland, when we found ourselves in South Carolina with a couple of days to spare. We phoned a professor of biology at a nearby college for directions to the Bachman's warbler habitat. He encouraged us to search in the Francis Beidler Forest. No recent sightings had occurred there, but he said the perfect habitat indicated a high probability that a pair of the warblers could breed there. What he did not tell us was that the forest lay at the end of a twenty-mile winding country road that forked away from a sandy county highway, far from the nearest town. And we were pulling a travel trailer behind our high-rise station wagon.

So we bumped along, car and small Airstream trailer, past small farms, vegetable gardens, and washing hanging out on lines to dry, and finally, at four o'clock in the afternoon, we arrived at the gate of the Francis Beidler Forest. An enormous chain across the entrance gate locked us out. A sign read OPEN 8 A.M. Obviously, if we wished to search for the rare warbler, we would have to return in the morning—much too late, to our way of thinking.

Our first inclination was to give up the search completely. There absolutely was no campground or county park in this region. Thoughts of the long, slow drive out and back again discouraged us from continuing the project we had been so keen to undertake. Leaning against our warm vehicle while attempting to make up our minds, we looked down the road at the little farms we had just passed. H-m-m. We reckoned that we would save hours of driving time if one of the farmers would allow us to park our camper on his property.

The very first neat little white house we approached was set in the center of a large yard, actually at the edge of the forest. A small child was playing there and informed us that his daddy wasn't home but his mommy was. She answered our query: "I'd like to let you park here, but Mr. Tom owns this place, and I wouldn't want to say yes without askin' him."

We drove into the driveway of the adjacent lot and knocked on the door of a freshly painted home set back on the property, leaving plenty of space for parking a trailer. A young man answered, "I wouldn't mind you stayin' overnight, but my dad is Mr. Tom, and I'd have to ask him first."

So we progressed from one little farm to another, all the occupants deferring to Mr. Tom.

At last we reached Mr. Tom's place, an old rambling house half hidden among trees, alongside which rippled a trout stream. Across the road from his home we enviously noted a wide, flat grassy area, a perfect trailer park. Mrs. Tom emerged just as a truck slammed into the driveway and another son joined the discussion. I slumped lower in the front seat of our station wagon, trying to hide my worn jeans and wrinkled hand-me-down blue oxford cloth shirt, which formerly belonged to one of my sons.

Mr. Tom's boy said, "I think we'd better check with pa. He's fishing up the river. I'll go ask him." Soon he returned, and so did Mr. Tom. Mr. Tom looked at our rig, then at my husband, and while we held our breath he made his proclamation. "You wouldn't want to camp out there. Follow me."

He climbed into the truck, and we followed him to a farm track along the edge of a garden, then across a field, circling a grassy meadow, until he stopped beside a little bridge, a lovely brook, and a canopy of trees filled with darting, melodious birds. The little glen would be our home for the night.

Mr. Tom shook our hands and wished us a good night. "You seemed like nice people," he commented simply. As the sunset painted a rosy glow over the horizon, we felt at peace with the world.

We think Mr. Tom's kind are Nice People.

PART IX

FAVORITE BIRD STORIES

A VERY LONELY WINTER WREN

Jean Piatt, in his book *Adventures in Birding: Confessions of a Lister,* wrote that every birder ought to have a small woods near his or her home, a place that he or she can visit in all seasons. I have been lucky to have such a magical place only a fifteen-minute drive from my home: Lakeport State Park in St. Clair County, Michigan, to which I fled almost daily during the times of spring and fall bird migration (fled from housework, that is).

It was a day in the middle of June, and my interest lay in which breeding birds had returned to their favorite spots. Would I hear the mourning warbler's "cheery cheery," or the "kuk kuk kuk" of the black-billed cuckoo? Suddenly I stopped in surprise—shock, actually—as the tinkling, rippling song of a winter wren floated out from a faraway corner of the park, whose border adjoined land owned by a church and a parochial school.

I had often walked along the edge of that patch of forest, but there were no trails leading into it. I carefully parted the sumac and prickly blackberry bushes and made my way under the maple, oak, and birch canopy, until I stumbled into a small glen. Fallen trees lay crisscrossed on the leafy forest floor. Moss covered the exposed roots. It was cool, dark, and damp.

I sat down on a fallen log. The tinkling song resumed, and soon the tiny brown bird, oblivious to my presence, was hurrying about, poking into the end of a hollow log, flicking around fallen branches, or skipping onto an exposed rock. I watched him for an hour or more, presuming I would soon see his mate.

As soon as I returned to the woods the next day, the rich, wild song guided me back to the glen. While the trills and cadences thrilled me, I knew that this southern Michigan county was way off the territorial limits of the winter wren. I had heard their songs in Alaska and Maine, and the range maps indicated breeding records all across northern Canada. But where was his mate?

Every day throughout the month of June, I visited the enchanted circle and was always led to it by the remarkable song. I say remarkable because the bird is so tiny and his brilliant refrain so ventriloquial. In July, I continued to stop by two or three times a week, partly out of curiosity and partly because I felt sorry for my little friend, who needed someone to sit nearby and admire his efforts at nest-building, and watch as he collected spiders and grubs from under logs and from the plentiful supply of woodland insects.

Then one day in early August, as I walked into the park I heard horrendous noises that turned out to be from chainsaws ripping at the large trees scattered across the back lawn of the church. "What is going on here?" I asked one of the workmen. "The church is going to create a prayer garden," was the reply.

I sat down in my usual place and asked the wren, "What do

you think of this?" For by now we were on very friendly terms. He cocked his head and looked at me with his dark eyes, then hopped upon a mossy log and went back to work. My heart was heavy as I walked away.

August fifteenth was my last visit. Hot flames from the burning tree trunks spiraled into the air and precluded any advance toward the woods. My winter wren had been driven from his woodland refuge by clouds of dark, enveloping smoke. I was too.

THE GOLDEN EAGLE OF DENALI

Such a tiny speck in the sky! From a distance it was difficult to identify the all-dark body and enormous wingspan, but it was surely a golden eagle, a bird to be expected in Denali National Park in Alaska.

That June day the clouds that ordinarily shroud the top of Mt. McKinley had lifted, and exposed the famous snowy cap of the mountain. Since no private vehicles are allowed on the ninety-mile highway that connects the park headquarters to the last campground, Wonder Lake, at the north edge of the park, I had departed with my birding group on the early-morning bus run. Chattering tourists excitedly pointed to the Dall sheep cropping grass on the alpine hillsides, or a baby moose grazing alongside its mother at the edge of a mossy bog, or sometimes in the distance a shuffling, shaggy grizzly bear.

Stops at the Savage River and Sanctuary campgrounds claimed a few backpackers; then the bus stopped at the base of Sable Mountain and we piled out. Our goal was to view a nesting surfbird at the very summit. How strange that a bird should

APPENDIX

TRAVEL RECORD

June–Aug. 1959	Norway	family trip
Aug. 1959	England	family trip
Aug. 1959	Scotland	family trip
July–Aug. 1964	Switzerland	int'l Scout session at Our Chalet
July 1966	Iceland	camping
May 1967	Greece	1st Ornithological Tour; R. T. Peterson
Apr.–May 1969	Greece	2nd Ornithological Tour
June–July 1970	Norway	family trip
Aug. 1970	Sweden	family trip
Jan. 1972	Mexico	birding with Peter Alden
1973	Alaska & St. Lawrence Island	family trip
1977	Attu Island	1st exploratory trip
1978	Attu Island	1st Larry Balch tour
May–June 1980	St. Lawrence Island	
1981	Chile	
Jan.–Feb. 1981	Circumnavigation of Antarctica	
Feb. 1981	New Zealand	

Mar. 1981	Australia	
Mar. 1981	Papua New Guinea	
Mar. 1981	Hawaii	
1981	Attu Island & St. Lawrence Island	
Feb.–Mar. 1982	Tanzania	birding with Peter Alden
Apr. 1983	Costa Rica	Talamanca rain forest
Mar. 1983	Panama	
May–June 1983	Attu Island	
Jan.–Feb. 1984	Peru	VENT tour with Ted Parker
May–June 1984	Attu Island	
Dec. 1984	Venezuela	birding with Kenn Kaufman
Jan. 1985	Costa Rica	VENT Christmas count
Feb. 1985	Thailand	
Feb. 1985	Burma	
Feb. 1985	Hong Kong	
Mar. 1985	Malaya	private tour
Mar. 1985	Philippines	R&R with Guy Howard
1985	Alaska	Kelly Bar
Oct. 1985	Brazil	
Oct. 1985	Paraguay	WINGS tour with Davis Finch
Oct. 1985	Argentina	
Mar. 1986	Cuba	Ontario Naturalists
May–June 1986	Attu Island & St. Lawrence Island	
July 1986	Mexico	preconference field trip
Jan. 1987	Jamaica	Ocho Rios
Feb. 1987	Venezuela	Tepius; VENT camping tour with Ted Parker
May 1987	Puerto Rico	with Ro Wauer
Aug. 1987	Namibia	
Sept. 1987	Botswana	VENT tour with Rhett Butler
Sept. 1987	Zimbabwe	

Sept. 1987	Zambia	with the Ndulo family
Sept.–Nov. 1987	Cameroon	Lutheran Mission
Mar. 1988	Mexico	
May 1988	West China	with Ben King
May 1988	Hong Kong	
Sept. 1988	Madagascar	
Sept. 1988	Mauritius Island	
Sept. 1988	Reunion Island	
Sept. 1988	Kenya	interval to meet Phoebe Snetsinger (private safari)
Oct. 1988	Zambia	with Phoebe Snetsinger & guide
Oct. 1988	Malawi	
Oct.–Nov. 1989	Australia	outback camping with Phil Maher
Jan. 1990	Morocco	Bird Bonanzas tour
Oct. 1990	Hawaii	early anniversary trip
Jan.–Feb. 1991	India	with Ben King
Feb. 1991	Andaman Islands	
Mar. 1991	Majorca	
Aug. 1991	Kenya	50th wedding anniv. family trip
Nov. 1991	Argentina	Field Guides tour
Jan. 1992	Belize	
May 1992	Caucasus Mountains, Southern Russia, following the Marco Polo trail to Tajikistan	Birdquest tour (British)
June 1992	Mongolia (Bill)	with Ben King
Mar. 1992	Oaxaca Chiapas	WINGS tour
Jan. 1993	New Zealand	private trip
Jan. 1993	Fiji	private trip
July 1993	Galapagos	
Mar. 1994	Bolivia	Field Guides tour with Roseanne Rowlett
Oct. 1994	South Africa	private tour

Mar. 1995	South Atlantic on *Professor Khromov,* to South Africa	
Mar. 1995	Tristan da Cunha & Nightingale Island	
Feb. 1996	Venezuela	WINGS tour (fishing camp)
Mar. 1996	Dominican Republic	WINGS tour
Apr. 1996	Lesser Antilles cruise	Bird Bonanzas tour on sailboat
Nov. 1997	Sub-Antarctic Islands off New Zealand; Snares Island	
Dec. 1997	Australia	McCarron's resort for Christmas
Feb. 2000	Philippines	with Ben King
July–Aug. 2000	Galapagos Islands	family trip
May 2001	Sweden	family trip
June 2002	Ireland	family trip
Dec.–Jan. 2002–3	Torremolinos, Spain	
Sept. 2003	Sweden	
Dec.–Jan. 2003–4	Torremolinos, Spain	
Nov. 2004	Turkey	
Dec.–Jan. 2004–5	Panama	

Made in the USA
Lexington, KY
11 December 2011